# A Gaia **Busy Person's** Guide

# Chakras

D1502333

A Gaia **Busy Person's** Guide

# Chakras

## Finding balance and serenity in everyday life

**Brenda Rosen**

Gaia Books

*Reconnect with yourself and the planet*

First published in Great Britain in 2007 by Gaia Books
a division of Octopus Publishing Group Ltd
2–4 Heron Quays, London E14 4JP.

Distributed in the United States and Canada by
Sterling Publishing Co., Inc.
387 Park Avenue South, New York, NY 10016–8810

ISBN-13:  978-185675-274-9
ISBN-10:  1-85675-274-7

A CIP catalogue record of this book is available from the British Library.

Printed and bound in China

10 9 8 7 6 5 4 3 2 1

**CAUTION**
*This book is not intended to
replace medical care under
the direct supervision of
a qualified doctor. Before
embarking on any changes in
your health regime, consult
your doctor. While all the
techniques detailed in this
book are extremely safe if
done correctly, you must
seek professional advice if
you are in any doubt about
any medical condition.*

# Contents

# Introducing chakras

You already know that, in addition to its physical parts, your body has energy. On some days, your energy is high and clear. You find it easy to concentrate, to accomplish complicated tasks effortlessly, and you flow easily from one activity to the next through your busy day. On other days, your energy feels sluggish or even blocked. Even the simplest task seems difficult, and you feel confused, distracted, or disconnected.

The flow of energy within the body is, of course, linked to your emotions and to physical factors, such as hormones and brain chemistry. However, even the most sophisticated medical measurements cannot account for how scattered and spaced out you feel on low energy days and how centred and relaxed you feel on days of high energy and easy flow.

To understand the subtle ebb and flow of body energy, it's necessary to look beyond Western medicine. For thousands of years, Eastern religious traditions such as Hinduism and Buddhism have taught that in addition to a physical body, you have an energy body. The anatomy of your energy body does not show up on an x-ray or a scan. Yet, as you'll discover in this book, the flow of life energy through the centres and channels of your energy body affects your physical health, your thoughts, your emotions, and your spiritual well-being. Many widely accepted alternative healing techniques, such as acupuncture, reflexology, and colour therapy, as well as the well-documented health benefits of yoga and meditation, are based not on the Western medical model but on the Eastern understanding of the energy body.

**TUNING IN**
*Relax and tune into your physical sensations, feelings, and thoughts to get in touch with your energy body.*

Moreover, it is possible to learn to regulate the flow of energy within your body by bringing attention to the seven energy centres aligned along the body's main energy channel. These seven centres are the chakras. The word *chakra* comes from Sanskrit and means disk or wheel. Intuitive healers, yoga practitioners, and experienced meditators describe the chakras as colourful swirling disks or wheels of life energy. As you'll discover, the chakras link your body's energy to the major concerns of your life – your physical survival, sexuality, ambition, and drive; your feelings of compassion and love; your ability to communicate; your imagination and spirituality.

**MEDITATION**
*Regular meditation practice can help you regulate the flow of energy through your chakras.*

## YOGA AND THE INDIAN TRADITION

If you have ever taken a yoga class, you know that *yoga*, a Sanskrit word that means union or joining, is a comprehensive health system aimed at joining the body, mind, and spirit. Physical postures and breathing exercises, combined with a healthy diet and lifestyle, relaxation, and meditation techniques are used to help regulate the flow of energy through the body's chakras and energy channels.

Yoga is very old. The philosophy that lies behind the modern practice of yoga dates back at least 5000 years to the ancient Hindu scriptures known as the *Vedas* and the *Upanishads*. About 2000 years ago, a Hindu scholar named Patanjali wrote the *Yoga Sutras*, a collection of wise sayings that lay out the eight limbs or aspects of yoga practice. These include good moral conduct, physical exercises, breathing practices, concentration and meditation. The aim of yoga is to help you feel harmonious, integrated, and complete within yourself despite the conflicting demands of your busy life.

Many of the techniques you'll learn in this book for working with your chakras are based on the principles of yoga. Like yoga practice, working with your chakras helps you to feel more balanced and centred, more calm, focused, and at ease. As you learn to regulate your body's energy flow, you discover different ways to release tension and stress and to improve your ability to concentrate. Working with the chakras also teaches you how to use your body's natural energy to relieve physical and emotional ills, increase passion and sexual satisfaction, and to deepen your ability to give and receive love. As you enhance energy flow to your upper

**LOTUS**
*Like the lotus floating
serenely above muddy water,
you can rise above difficulties
by learning to adjust your
body energy.*

chakras, you find your authentic voice and deepen your access to intuition and creative vision.

Most importantly, like yoga, working with your chakras helps you to develop a sense of wholeness and unity among the various aspects of your body and mind. As you harmonize your life energy with the energy that flows within all life, your spirituality deepens and you feel more at peace with yourself and with everything around you.

## USING THIS BOOK
This book is designed to offer you a wide variety of methods for accessing and regulating your body's energy throughout your busy day: as part of your morning routine, at work, as you relate to others, when you feel unwell, and as you prepare for sleep. You'll also learn about the special qualities of each chakra and how to use its energy to enhance your life.

**HATHA YOGA**
*Most yoga classes focus
on hatha yoga, a series
of postures designed to
harmonize the energies of
the body, mind, breath,
and spirit.*

# CHAPTER ONE

# Getting to know your chakras

The seven chakras are the body's energy stations. Each regulates an aspect of your personality and devotes its energy to important tasks. Learning to assess and regulate the flow of energy through these centres helps give you balance and harmony.

Working with your chakras will introduce you to a number of ideas that may be unfamiliar. Some of these concepts are drawn from Eastern beliefs. Luckily, today you live in a time in which the "secrets" of Eastern spiritual practice, including the understanding of the chakras presented in this book, are widely available and widely accepted.

In many ways, Western science is helping Eastern ideas to be better understood. Even if you know nothing else about modern physics, you probably know that its basis is the idea that energy and matter are really different forms of the same thing. The $c$ in Einstein's famous energy-matter equation ($e = mc^2$) is the speed of light. So, put another way, your body is simply light energy that has been slowed down or frozen into solid form!

Thus, learning to work with the body's energy is no more mystical than yoga or any other kind of physical exercise. You're simply giving your inner light a good workout and, as you do, enhancing your health, well-being, and happiness.

# Your energy body

It's easy to picture in your mind the network of arteries and veins that carry your blood throughout your body. Now imagine that there is a further network of branching pathways through which your life energy circulates. These pathways, called *nadis* in Hinduism and Buddhism, are far more subtle than the arteries and veins of your circulatory system.

The body's central energy pathway is a transparent, flexible tube, about the width of a drinking straw, often described as being made of light. Buddhist meditators call this pathway "the central channel" and describe it as pale blue on the outside and blood red on the inside. In yoga, this pathway is called the *sushumna*. It runs parallel to your spine, slightly in front of your backbone, from the chakra at the base of the spine to the chakra at the top of your head. From there, it curves slightly downward and terminates at the chakra located between your two eyebrows.

## SUN AND MOON NADIS

On the right and the left side of this main pathway are two smaller but important nadis. On the right is the sun channel or *pingala*. It is red in colour, masculine, and hot. It runs alongside the central channel, but at the upper end, it terminates at the right nostril. On the left is the moon channel or *ida*. White in colour, feminine and cool, it terminates at the left nostril. You might think of these channels as a superhighway with parallel roads on either side.

At key points along the central channel, the two side channels cross over the central channel forming an

**ENERGY ANATOMY**
*The right and left channels of the energy body twist around the central channel at each chakra point.*

energy intersection or chakra. At each intersection, life energy is collected and is processed and stored. From there, it flows to various parts of your body and mind. Your chakras are also receiving stations for energy from your environment and transmitters of your energy to your surroundings. For instance, the excited or aggressive energy you pick up from a crowd at a sports event or the peaceful energy you absorb during a walk through a forest comes into your body and is stored in one of the chakras.

### LIFE-GIVING PRANA

Life energy, called *Qi* in Chinese medicine and *prana* in yoga, is the life force that flows throughout your body, as it does through every living thing. Without it, you would not be alive. You absorb prana from the food you eat, the water you drink, and the air you breathe. Spending time in nature, breathing clean, unpolluted air as you exercise, as well as eating fresh, organic food nourishes your body with prana.

When the flow of your life energy is well balanced and your nadis are functioning smoothly, your physical energy, emotions, and thoughts work together in harmony. When your prana is out of balance, you may experience physical or emotional problems. For instance, an excess of prana in your upper chakras can make you feel restless, flighty, or ungrounded. Conversely, an excess of prana in the lower chakras can make you feel excessively self-centred, fearful, or suspicious. The smooth flow of prana through the nadis can also be impeded or blocked by emotional distress or physical illness.

*LIVING WATER*
*To nourish your body with life energy, try to drink 4–8 glasses of fresh spring water every day.*

The flow of life energy in to and out of your body, imbalances among your chakras, and blockages in your energy channels can often be seen in your aura. The aura is the colourful egg-shaped energy field that surrounds every living thing. Kirlian photographs taken with special cameras can capture the human aura on film. Psychics and healers can see the aura and use it to gain information about the flow and balance of a person's life energy.

***RECHARGE NATURALLY***
*Spending time in peaceful outdoor settings gives you the opportunity to recharge your life energy in a natural way.*

### THE SEVEN CHAKRAS

*The most important features of your energy body are the seven chakras aligned vertically along the central energy channel. Each chakra influences a particular aspect of your life. You will learn more about the function of each chakra in the chapters that follow, but to get you started, here is an overview.*

### The root chakra

*Located at base of your spine near your sexual organs, the task of the first chakra is to ensure your safety and survival. It influences your basic instincts and your ability to provide for life's necessities. It keeps you grounded and gives you a sense of stability and self-worth.*

### The sacral chakra

*Located about 8 cm (3 in) below your naval, the second chakra stimulates your sexuality and your creativity. Related to the sense of touch and to the need to nurture and be nurtured, it influences your perception of pleasure and pain and keeps your masculine and feminine qualities in balance.*

### The solar plexus chakra

*Located in the upper part of the abdomen between the chest and the naval, the third chakra is connected to your power, drive, will, and ambition. It influences your self-confidence and helps you take responsibility for making decisions. It is also the site of your basic intuition or "gut feelings".*

### The heart chakra

*Located in the centre of the chest, the fourth chakra is dedicated to love and compassion for yourself and others. It influences your ability to accept things as they are, to feel respect and empathy and to forgive. It also gives you the capacity to grieve.*

### The throat chakra

*Located at the throat, the fifth chakra governs your ability to express yourself. It is connected to your willingness to tell the truth and to your integrity. It directs your ability to make decisions, find the right career, and manifest your dreams.*

### The brow chakra

*Located between your eyebrows, the sixth chakra is connected to inspiration, intuition, and vision. Often called "the third eye", opening this chakra can bring psychic and spiritual gifts, such as clairvoyance and the capacity to channel healing energy. At its most developed, this chakra gives you access to wisdom.*

### The crown chakra

*Located at the top of the head, the seventh chakra is the gateway to the spiritual understanding that leads to enlightenment. It governs your ability to act in selfless or humanitarian ways, to experience faith and devotion, and to enter into spiritual peace, ecstasy, and bliss.*

### SENSING YOUR LIFE ENERGY

*With a little practice, you can learn to sense the energy of your chakras with your hands. If you don't feel anything during this exercise, or aren't sure, don't worry. Try the exercise again another day.*

*(01) Sit comfortably or lie on your back on a yoga mat or blanket. Spend a few minutes watching your breath, following it all the way in and all the way out.*

*(02) Rub the palms of your hands together briskly for about 30 seconds. Then open your hands to about 45 cm (18 in) apart, then slowly bring your palms toward each other. When your palms are about 10 cm (4 in) apart, you should be able to feel the tingling of your own life energy between your hands.*

01

02

03

04

*(03) Now rub your hands together again briskly for 30 seconds and hold your hands about 8–10 cm (3–4 in) away from your body above the sacral chakra, located 8 cm (3 in) below your naval. Tune in closely and see what you feel.*

*(04) Experiment with placing your hands above the heart chakra in the middle of your chest, above the throat chakra, and then above the brow chakra between your eyebrows. Note what you feel. Also pay attention to any colours, sounds, words, or images that come to your mind as you sense the energy of each chakra.*

# Chakra connections

In addition to their connection to major areas of your life, the seven chakras also correspond to elemental forces and colours. Each is associated with positive tasks and potential problems. Here is a general table

| CHAKRA | LOCATION | COLOUR | ELEMENT | |
|---|---|---|---|---|
| Root | Base of spine, near genitals | Red | Earth | |
| Sacral | Below navel | Orange | Water | |
| Solar plexus | Upper abdomen | Yellow | Fire | |
| Heart | Centre of chest | Green | Air | |
| Throat | Neck | Blue | Sound | |
| Brow | Between the eyebrows | Indigo | Light | |
| Crown | Top of the head | Violet | Spirit | |

showing these chakra connections. You'll find more
information about these correspondences and
methods for strengthening the positive qualities
of each chakra in the chapters that follow.

| POSITIVE TASKS | POTENTIAL PROBLEMS |
|---|---|
| Survival, stability, grounding, ability to stand up for yourself, good judgment, self-worth | Depression, lack of self-confidence, low self-esteem, risk-taking, addictions, disappointment with life |
| Sexual pleasure, flexibility, ability to generate new ideas, ability to nurture and be nurtured | Rigidity and inflexibility, lack of desire and sexual satisfaction, fear of touch and intimacy, abuse and self-neglect |
| Power, prosperity, will, drive, ambition, responsibility, gut feelings | Fatigue, lack of ambition and drive, misuse of power, anger, tendency to blame others, resentment, guilt |
| Ability to love and be loved, empathy, compassion, acceptance, forgiveness, ability to grieve | Loneliness, critical judgment, difficult relationships, passive-aggressive behaviour, pessimism |
| Ability to speak, ability to listen, integrity, creative and artistic self-expression, wit and humour | Lack of communication skills, lying, taking yourself too seriously, blocked creativity |
| Inspiration, intuition, intelligence, vision, insight, wisdom | Lack of clarity, lack of follow through, lack of perception and insight, learning disabilities |
| Faith, spirituality, peace, ecstasy, bliss, mystical understanding, enlightenment | Confusion, spiritual pride, lack of faith, arrogance, spiritual scepticism |

# Working with your chakras

This book provides you with a wealth of exercises and practices for working with your chakras. Some are physical exercises for your body and breath drawn from yoga and related disciplines. Others are inner work exercises, such as journaling, drawing, visualizations, and meditations. Many people find that beginning a session with a movement or breath exercise helps them to relax and makes it easier to engage in journaling, meditation, or other inner work.

Setting up a regular time for working with your chakras can help you in many ways. A regular schedule eliminates the need to find time each day for personal work. As a minimum, try to spend ten minutes in the morning and ten minutes before bed working with the practices in this book. Ideally, you should be private and uninterrupted as you work, so close the

## EQUIPMENT
*You'll find the following supplies useful for the exercises in this book:*
- *A yoga mat or blanket for floor exercises*
- *A journal or notebook*
- *Several large sheets of drawing paper*
- *A pen*
- *Coloured pencils, markers or other drawing supplies*

## PERSONAL ART
*Give yourself permission to experiment with coloured pencils, pens, and other art supplies, even if you think you can't draw.*

door to your room, turn off your mobile phone, and give yourself permission to focus solely on yourself.

You might wonder how movement and breathing exercises can influence your chakras. As you see in the Chakra Connections chart on pages 20–21, each chakra influences the energy of nearby parts of the body. For this reason, physical exercises that focus on related parts of the body affect the nearby chakra as well. Moreover, the rhythm of your breath is the closest physical equivalent to the movement of your subtle energy currents. As you have learned, the right and left energy channels terminate at the right and left nostrils. Thus breathing exercises can affect the movement of prana through your energy pathways.

## AIRS OR WINDS

*The body's subtle energy currents are known as "airs" or "winds" in some Eastern spiritual systems.*

# Visualizing your chakras

Creating a visual representation of your chakras is a useful way to find out what you already know about your energy body.

In personal art exercises like chakra drawing, the process is more important than the finished artwork. Drawing, sketching, and doodling allow you to access deeper levels of understanding than language alone. Though you may not be able to explain in words your impression of a particular chakra, choosing a colour and drawing a symbol or image for it can give you helpful insights.

For instance, drawing a tight scribble of bright red lines at your solar plexus chakra may hint at anger you have been unwilling or unable to express. Drawing your solar plexus as a bright yellow sun with beams extending beyond your body outline, on the other hand, may indicate that your basic approach to life is positive and optimistic.

Study the chart on pages 20–21 to get you started. Work quickly, without thinking too much about the meaning of what you are drawing. You can repeat this exercise as you continue to work with your chakras to see whether your perceptions have changed.

**CHAKRA DRAWING**

*1. Draw an outline of the human body. At the point on the drawing where the legs meet the body, draw an image or design that represents the energy of your root chakra using coloured pencils, markers, or other drawing materials. Choose colours and shapes that express the energetic feeling of this chakra for you. Draw any blocks or obstructions in your energy channels with lines or other shapes. If you wish, you can add words to your drawing that express the feeling of each chakra.*

*2. Now, in the space of your lower abdomen, draw an image or design that represents the energy of your sacral chakra using colours, shapes, and words that express your perception of this energy in your life.*

*3. Moving on to the space of your upper abdomen and draw an image or design that represents the energy of your solar plexus chakra.*

4. *Next, draw a symbol for the heart chakra in the middle of the chest, then the throat chakra on the neck, the brow chakra on the upper part of the face, and the crown chakra at the top of the head.*

5. *When your picture seems complete, look at it as a whole. Which chakras are larger and which are smaller? Which are the most colourful or most attractive? Which chakra seems the most troubled or difficult? What does your drawing reveal that you did not know? What areas of your life does it indicate need the most attention? If you have gained any insights from the exercise that seem important, record them in your journal.*

# Breath work

You'll get the greatest benefit from a session of chakra work when you are centred and relaxed. Focusing on the breath, as in this meditation drawn from Buddhist practice, is a great way to begin. It helps to release any tension, clear the mind, and flush stale energy from the nadis. Use it whenever you wish to feel calm and clear.

01

02

### NINE-ROUND BREATH MEDITATION

*(01) Sit comfortably on a chair or on the floor with your back straight. Tilt your head slightly downward, close your eyes or focus softly on a place on the floor about 1 m (3 ft) in front of you. Visualize the three main energy channels in your body (see p.12). Imagine that the right channel and left channel are joined at a point about 8 cm (3 in) below your navel.*

*(02) Place your index finger against your nose to close off your left nostril. Breathe in through your right nostril. Imagine you are inhaling pure white light, which travels from the right nostril into the right energy channel all the way down to the point below your navel where the right and left channel meet.*

*(03) Now move your index finger so that it closes off your right nostril and exhale slowly and fully through the left nostril, imagining that you are breathing out all blockages and impurities. Imagine that these exit your body in the form of black smoke, leaving your left channel clean and luminous. Repeat this process two more times.*

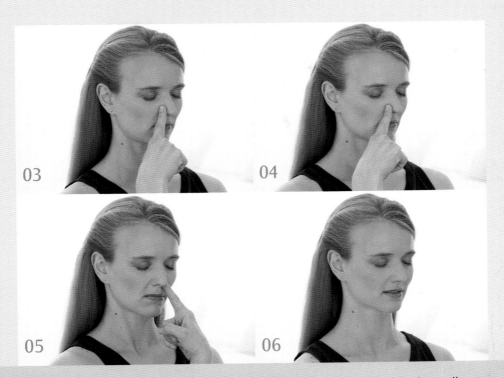

03

04

05

06

*(04) Next, close off your right nostril with your index finger and inhale pure white light through your left nostril. Follow the air all the way down your left channel to the point below your navel where the right and left channels join.*

*(05) Now close off your left nostril again and breathe out any obstructions in your right channel. Imagine they exit your body through the right nostril in the form of thick black smoke, leaving your right channel clean and luminous. Repeat this clearing process two more times.*

*(06) Finally, inhale through both nostrils imagining that you are inhaling pure white cleansing light. Follow the light all the way down to the point below your navel where you imagine that the tips of the right and left channels have been inserted into the central channel. As you exhale through both nostrils, imagine that the light clears all blockages and stale air from the central channel. These leave your body from the upper end of the central energy channel located between your eyebrows in the form of thick black smoke. Repeat this process two more times for a total of nine rounds.*

# Full body relaxation

Yoga is another good preparation for chakra work. The full-body relaxation pose explained here, called the "corpse pose" or *savasana* in yoga, is deceptively simple. Though it may seem easy to lie on the floor with your eyes closed, this pose can be surprisingly difficult at first. Your body may move around restlessly and your busy mind may distract you from being able to relax completely. Here, too, focusing on your breathing can help your mind and body settle into relaxation more easily.

**CORPSE POSE**

*1. Lie down on the floor on a yoga mat or blanket. If it will make you more comfortable, place a flat pillow under your head. Stretch out your legs and rest your arms near your sides, palms facing up. Close your eyes. Raise your buttocks briefly and lengthen your lower back so that as much of your spine as possible is resting on the floor. Allow your feet to relax completely and flop out to the sides.*

**AROMATHERAPY**
*Place a few drops of a calming scented oil, such as sandalwood, bergamot, neroli, or lavender in an oil burner as another aid to releasing stress and tension.*

*2. Bring your attention to your breath and imagine that you are breathing with your whole body, from the crown of your head to the tips of your toes. Allow every muscle in your body to relax.*

*3. As you relax, imagine your body softening and sinking into the floor. Stay in this state of relaxed awareness for as long as you like.*

*4. To exit this pose, start to breathe more deeply, stretch your legs, then your arms. Roll onto one side and sit up.*

# CHAPTER TWO

# Starting the day

How do you start your day? Do you jump up before the alarm or do you need ten drowsy minutes in bed before facing the day? Your morning style is related to a combination of physical and energy body factors.

While the exercises in this chapter will not transform a slow-starter into a morning go-getter, they can help you create a personal morning energy routine that will harmonize with your natural rhythms.

Taking time each morning to wake up your energy body has positive benefits throughout the day – when your energies are humming, you feel more vibrant and alive. You think more clearly and make better choices. You find that doing physical activities, such as a brisk walk to the bus stop or an early morning jog, vitalize and strengthen you. Moreover, it's easier to maintain good health, as a well-balanced energy body boosts your immune system.

In this chapter are creative ways to clear, strengthen, and balance your seven chakras each morning. In addition, you will find suggestions for giving special attention to the root chakra at the base of your spine. The job of the root chakra is to create a strong foundation for your life and to help you stay balanced, centred, and grounded throughout your busy day. Exercises that strengthen your root chakra provide the stability you require to accomplish everything you need to do.

# Awakening your energy body

You can begin awakening your energy body before you even get out of bed. Lightly touching each chakra with your mind and breath helps to brush away sleep cobwebs and open your body and spirit to the day's new possibilities.

Like the breath, thoughts are a form of energy. Guiding your attention to various parts gently infuses your body with thought energy, harmonizing body and mind and grounding your conscious awareness in your physical form. You can use a similar technique whenever tension or fatigue makes you feel confused or disconnected. Guide your mind to your root chakra and breathe into it until you feel steady.

**WHEN YOU WAKE UP**
*Do this exercise either lying on a yoga mat or blanket or sitting in your favourite chair with a morning cup of tea.*

*1. Take a few deep conscious breaths to help focus your attention inward, then gently allow your mind to travel to your root chakra at the base of your spine. Breathe consciously for a minute or two, inviting the grounding and stabilizing energy of your first chakra to awaken.*

*2. Now guide your mind upward along the central channel to the sacral chakra below your navel. As you breathe, invite this chakra to awaken you to the possibilities of flexibility and pleasure.*

*3. Now guide your mind upward to the solar plexus chakra located between your ribcage and navel. Lightly touch it with consciousness as you breathe and invite its power and drive to invigorate your day ahead.*

4. Allow your consciousness to travel upward to the heart chakra at the centre of your chest. Feel a warm rush of loving-kindness for yourself and others as your breathing gently invites your heart centre to awaken.

5. Move your mind upward to your throat chakra at the front of your neck. As you breathe, allow a sound or a word to form in your mind. Say the word aloud if it feels right or note it mentally as a keynote of your day.

6. Guide your mind upward to awaken the brow chakra between your eyebrows. As you breathe, invite intuition and insight into your day.

7. Finally, move your consciousness to the crown chakra at the top of your head. As this centre awakens, acknowledge your connection with everything that is.

**MORNING TEA**
You don't need to lie down to awaken your chakras. Simply turn your attention inside and focus briefly on each energy centre as you sip your morning tea.

# Energizing and smoothing your aura

Even if you don't see auras, you can probably feel them. Isn't there someone in your life – perhaps your boss or your partner's mother – whose energy you can sense before you see the person?

The same is true about you. If you want others to welcome your energetic presence, take time in the morning to energize and repair your aura. Doing so helps to smooth out disturbances and weaves a field of protection around you.

**AURA COMBING**

*(01) Stand comfortably with your feet a shoulder-width apart.*

*(02) Gently bend forward from your waist. Beginning at your feet, roll the energy of your aura upward by circling your hands 7–10 cm (3–4 in) away from your body as if you were rolling a soft ball up the front of your body. Your palms should be facing toward you as your hands circle each other. Breathe deeply, allowing your breath to give your aura space to expand, like fluffing up a feather pillow.*

01

02

(03) Continue to roll the energy up your legs until you reach the site of your root chakra. Circle your hands here for a moment or two. You may find that your hands spontaneously move farther away from your body at a chakra point or else move closer to dip more deeply into your energy field.With practice, you'll learn to sense disturbances in your aura. A chakra site where there is too little energy may feel hollow. A sudden rush of energy might signal a tear in your field. Or the previously smooth flow of energy might feel constricted or blocked at a certain point.

(04) If you sense that something in your field needs repair, spend a few minutes circling your hands 7–10 cm (3–4 in) away from the spot. Trust that your hands know how to fix things using kneading, scooping, or smoothing motions. Continue until you sense that the energy is flowing harmoniously.

(05) Continue circling your hands up the front of your body pausing at each of your chakras to energize, smooth, or repair. Experiment with slow and fast movements, long and short strokes. End above the crown of your head.

03     04     05

# Cleansing your chakras with light

As you have read, your chakras and energy channels are often described as being made of light energy. As you may also know, white light is really a mixture of colours, called a spectrum. A glass prism, a crystal drop hanging in a window, or the raindrops in a sunny sky that create a rainbow reveal that the seven main colours of the light spectrum are red, orange, yellow, green, blue, indigo, and violet.

It won't surprise you to discover that these same seven colours are associated with the chakras. As you see on the chart on pages 20–21, each chakra vibrates in harmony with one of the colours of the rainbow spectrum. The colours progress in a logical sequence from the lowest frequency to the highest. The root, sacral, and solar plexus chakras vibrate at the slower frequencies of red, orange, and yellow light. The heart, throat, brow, and crown chakras vibrate more quickly – or, you might say, have more energy – to harmonize with green, blue, indigo, and violet light.

**NATURAL PRISM**
*A raindrop sparkling on a green leaf refracts sunlight into rainbow colours like a natural prism.*

**CRYSTAL DROP**
*A crystal drop hanging in a sunny window creates an ever-changing play of delightful light and colour.*

Colour therapy is also becoming a more widely accepted method of complementary healing. In colour therapy, the body is bathed in coloured light, coloured gemstones are placed on the chakras, or coloured light is visualized as pouring into each of the chakras. You actually experience a simple form of colour therapy when wearing a bright red sweater makes you feel sexy, or sitting in a room with pale blue walls calms your emotions. You also practise colour therapy when you arrange a vase of flowers. You'll learn more about colour healing and using gemstones in Chapter five.

### COLOUR HEALING
*Psychic healers and others who see auras can often diagnose problems by sensing disruptions in the chakras' rainbow colour pattern.*

## CLEANSING AND BALANCING

The meanings associated with colours change with time and culture. In many Asian cultures, red symbolizes happiness, marriage, and prosperity, while mourners at a funeral wear white. Many Native American cultures attach sacred meanings to the colours black, yellow, red, and white, associating each with one of the directions on the compass. In Europe, purple is the colour of royalty.

The association of particular colours with the chakras probably comes from ancient India. In this visualization exercise, a rainbow of colours will cleanse and balances your chakras. As you gain experience with using colour in your chakra work, you'll develop your own personal associations with particular hues.

1. Sit comfortably in a chair, with your back straight and your feet flat on the floor. Allow your eyes to close and take a few conscious breaths, following your breathing all the way in and all the way out. Imagine that a bright ball of white light is floating just above your head. Remind yourself that white light actually contains a spectrum of colours.

2. Reach with your mind into the ball of white light and draw out the colour red. A stream of red light enters your crown chakra and travels down the central channel until it reaches your root chakra. Your root chakra is filled with red light, strengthening and balancing its energy.

3. Now from the ball of white light, draw out a stream of orange light. The orange light travels down the centre of your body to the sacral chakra, filling you with vitality.

4. Next, draw golden yellow light from the white ball and bring it down to your solar plexus chakra. Feel the golden light fill the centre of your body and spread outward, warming you from within.

5. Draw green light from the white ball and bring it down to your heart chakra. As the light fills the centre of your chest, feel a warm rush of tenderness and love for both yourself and others.

6. Draw bright blue light from the white ball to fill your throat chakra. This light will help to strengthen its energy, giving you the capacity to speak clearly and to listen deeply to yourself and others.

7. Now indigo light – a deep, purplish-blue – streams from the white ball into your brow chakra, cleansing the window of your inner vision and strengthening your intuition.

8. Finally, cool violet light streams from the white ball into your crown chakra, and you glimpse peace, ecstasy, and bliss. Check mentally that each chakra is filled with its appropriate colour. Acknowledge that this rainbow of light has strengthened and balanced your energy body.

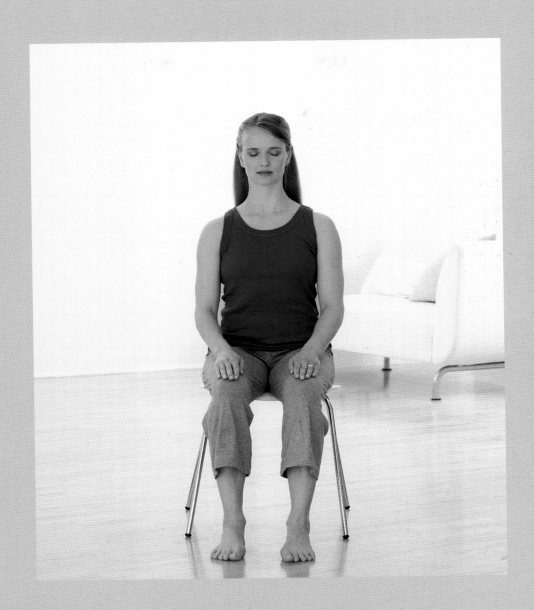

# Breath of life

Your energy and your breath are deeply connected. In yoga, postures that focus on the breath are called *pranayama*. Prana is the life force energy that flows through your chakras and channels (see pages 12–15). Pranayama exercises, in which you use your mind and body to control your breathing, have many practical benefits. They bring oxygen to your cells, increasing your vitality and improving your mental focus. They also invigorate the flow of life force energy.

**COMPLETE BREATHING**

*This simple breathing exercise, called in yoga Complete Breath Standing, is a great technique to include in your morning energy routine.*

*(01) Stand with your feet slightly apart, in line with your shoulders. Your arms should hang loosely at your sides. Gently focus your mind inward and follow your breathing for a few minutes until you feel relaxed.*

*(02) Exhale slowly and completely through your nose. Pull in your stomach muscles as you*

01      02      03

breathe out to make sure you have exhaled completely. Focus for an instant on the gap between the exhalation and the inhalation.

(03) Inhale slowly and with control. As you inhale, allow your arms to float upward, with your palms facing the ceiling. Expand your chest and relax your diaphragm so that you inhale as much air as possible.

(04) At the end of your inhalation, your arms should be outstretched above your head, with your palms touching.

(05) Gently hold your breath as you mentally count to five. Then breathe out with control, slowly lowering your arms, with palms facing toward the floor, until you have exhaled completely and your arms are hanging relaxed at your sides.

(06) Repeat this sequence for five complete breaths. Try to keep your attention focused on how your physical movements affect your breathing throughout the exercise. If you find that your mind wanders, gently bring it back to your sensations.

04  05  06

# Centring through journal writing

Spending five minutes in the morning writing in a journal is a good way to centre yourself and set your intentions for the day ahead. A personal journal is just that – personal! No one will read what you write. No teacher will correct your spelling. Journaling in the morning is an opportunity for you to pay attention to your thoughts and feelings and to get your energy moving in the direction of your goals and dreams.

There are many ways to keep a journal. If you've never tried journaling or want to make journaling part of your morning energy routine, here is an easy way to get started.

Open your journal to a fresh page, write the date at the top, then just write whatever comes into your mind. What you write does not need to make sense or have any order. Ignore the need to use correct spelling, punctuation, or grammar. Ignore the need to write neatly, so long as you'll be able to read what you've written later on, if you wish. Keep writing continuously for five minutes, even if you think you have nothing to say. For example, write:

*I have nothing to say. I have nothing to write. This is silly. My mind is a blank. I wonder whether Jim will call me? Why am I thinking about Jim again? Thinking about Jim makes me angry. What are my goals? What do I need to do today? I have to remember to stop at the cleaners. I must phone Anne about next Saturday. What else? I want to remember to stay calm when things get hectic at work. I intend to order a salad at lunch and to get to yoga class tonight.*

**PERSONAL JOURNAL**
*If you've never tried keeping a personal journal or diary, the journaling exercises that you'll find throughout this book are a good way to get you started.*

# Special focus: the root chakra

The Sanskrit name for the root chakra is *muladhara*, which means "root". Like a tree, you need strong roots to keep you safe and well grounded. The energy of the first chakra moves downward – down from the base of your spine, through your legs and feet and into the element associated with the first chakra, which is earth.

Working with your root chakra energy means getting in touch with your basic needs – including everything you do to take care of your physical body, such as eating the right foods and making time for exercise. A well-functioning root chakra makes good self-care effortless, which in turn provides the emotional stability you need to accomplish everything that you need to do.

When your root chakra is healthy, it's easy to make wise decisions about where you live, how you manage your money, how you care for your home, and how you manage the details of your daily schedule. Health issues that threaten your stability, including addictions and immune system disorders, may be related to blockages or deficiencies in the root chakra.

Emotionally, a healthy root chakra helps you to set good boundaries in your relationships and to stand up for yourself by saying no when it is appropriate. It also improves your self-discipline and gives you the ability to finish what you start. Problems with your root chakra can make you excessively fearful of criticism and also rejection. When you don't take good care of yourself physically and emotionally, you may be perpetually in survival mode – always feeling that you are in danger even when there is no real threat.

The chart that follows suggests ways to strengthen and balance the energy of your root chakra. Working with your root chakra each morning helps you to create a firm foundation for your day and life.

### METHODS FOR STRENGTHENING YOUR ROOT CHAKRA

| Where to focus | What to do |
| --- | --- |
| Foods | Eat protein rich foods, such as meat or fish. |
| Colour therapy | Wear something red, such as a blouse, sweater, or scarf. |
| Aromatherapy | Put a few drops of an earthy essential oil in your morning bath, such as myrrh, patchouli, vetiver, or oakmoss. |
| Crystals | Carry a piece of bloodstone or smoky quartz in your pocket. |
| Clothes | Choose shoes that give you a firm foundation, avoiding high heels or backless sandals. |
| Self-care | Make an appointment for a check up with your doctor or dentist; give yourself a hand or foot massage; check your bank balance. |
| Recreation | Take a walk in the woods; sit with your back against a tree; work in the garden. |
| House and home | Clean out a drawer, kitchen cupboard, or wardrobe; make a needed repair. |
| Journal exercise | Write about: how well do I take care of myself? or, what can I do to feel more grounded and secure? |

## TREE MEDITATION

*This grounding and centring meditation uses the symbol of a tree to strengthen your root chakra.*

*1. Sit cross-legged on a yoga mat or blanket, or sit in a chair with your feet flat on the floor. Make sure your back is straight. Concentrate on your breathing.*

*2. Imagine that a strong root, like a tree root, is growing from the bottom of your spine and reaching down into the earth. Remind yourself that this root anchors you firmly to the ground, giving you the ability to provide for all of your needs.*

*3. Imagine that essential nourishment is flowing from the earth through this root to every part of your body. Remind yourself that healthy thoughts and feelings, like beautiful leaves and flowers, are made possible by the stability provided by this root.*

*4. When your meditation feels complete, spend a few minutes massaging your legs and feet.*

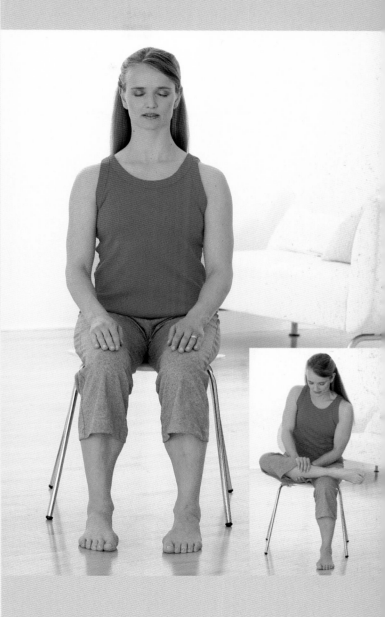

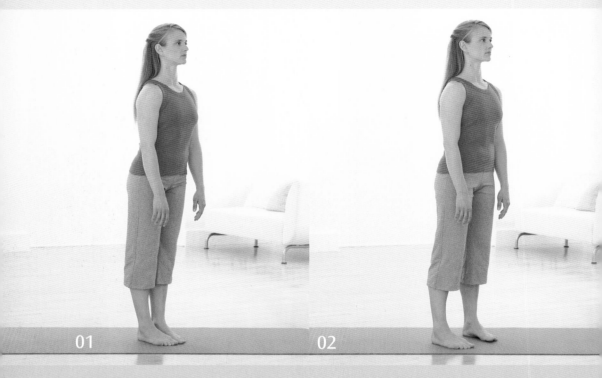

01    02

### MOUNTAIN POSE

*This yoga pose, called* tadasana, *strengthens your root chakra and helps you to feel as steady and secure as a mountain.*

*(01) Stand with your feet together. Close your eyes for a moment and focus your attention on the soles of your feet. Open your eyes and experiment with making adjustments to your feet so that they feel completely secure and balanced. If necessary, move your feet slightly apart, or shift your weight backward onto your heels or forward onto your toes*

*until you rest in a position that feels secure. Make sure that every part of your foot is in contact with the ground, from toe to heel and from inside edge to outside edge.*

*(02) Now move your attention upward to your legs. Bend your knees slightly to wake up your legs, then straighten them gently, making sure that your weight is evenly distributed over the balls of your feet. Also make sure that your knees are directly above your ankles and that your hips are directly above your knees.*

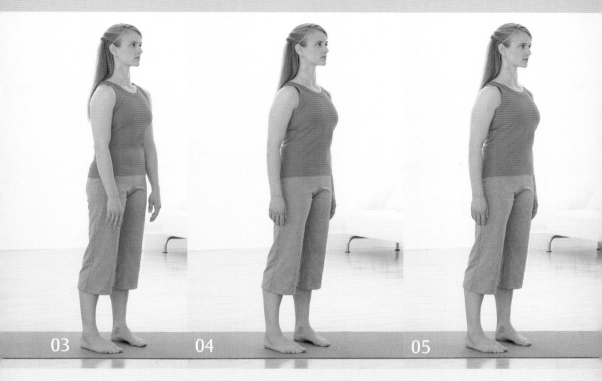

03          04                    05

(03) Now move your attention upwards to the area of the root chakra where your legs join your torso. Tuck in your tailbone and make sure that your buttocks are aligned evenly. Tighten and release your pelvic muscles a few times until this part of your body feels perfectly balanced.

(04) Expand the top of your chest and drop your shoulders, feeling the support of your spine through your neck. Allow your arms to hang loosely by your sides, with your palms facing toward your body.

(05) Relax your throat and drop your head slightly, allowing the back of your neck to lengthen. Rest for a few moments with the strong steadiness of a mountain, pressing down firmly with your feet and feeling the energy of the earth flowing upward through your channels and chakras.

# CHAPTER THREE

# Chakras at work

Whether your workday involves a commute to the office, household chores and childcare, travel and meetings, or some other kind of activity, a well-functioning energy body can help you meet its demands.

Every kind of work you do involves an exchange of energy. Talking to a co-worker, writing a report, shopping, doing laundry, interacting with your children, or travelling on a plane require that you either expend your own energy or take in the energy of others. Working with your chakras helps you to become aware of your everyday energy exchanges and teaches you to manage your energy in a healthy way.

Managing your energy at work also means developing awareness of the ebb and flow of your energy level over the course of your workday so that you can make needed adjustments. In this chapter you'll find a number of exercises focused on the solar plexus chakra that you can use to boost your energy when you are feeling depleted, release tension and stress, and focus your will, vitality and sense of purpose on completing the task at hand.

Almost all work involves communication, which is governed by the throat chakra. It's easy to see that the throat chakra is involved when you speak. But the throat chakra also influences your ability to listen attentively, to write, and to communicate through body language. Even reading an email draws on throat chakra energy.

Strengthening the energies of your solar plexus and throat chakras, as you'll learn to do in this chapter, helps you to work with power, focus, and clarity and to communicate clearly and articulately.

# Energy exchanges

At every moment in your workday, you are exchanging energy. Sometimes the exchange of energy is very obvious, such as when you are engaged in a heated conversation with a colleague. Other energy exchanges are less obvious. If you commute to work on public transport, you may exchange energy with hundreds of strangers before you even reach your office!

You also exchange energy with objects and places. Your office furniture, the colours of the walls and fixtures, and the plants and pictures on your desk

**COMMUNICATION**
*Making a presentation gives your communication chakra, the throat chakra, a workout. Every single word, gesture, and facial expression draws on throat chakra energy.*

all have a subtle effect on your energy. Places also transmit and absorb energy. Think for a moment of how it feels to work in a sleek, glass and steel skyscraper as opposed to working in a factory where people have laboured for decades. The energy in old buildings is so complex because the structure has absorbed layers of energy from the many people who have spent time there.

Part of learning to work with your chakras is developing awareness so that you can adjust your

**URBAN ENERGY**
*It is easy to see the vibrant energy of a modern city, but every place people live and work has its own unique energy pattern.*

energy as needed. Your solar plexus chakra is a source of basic intuition – what is more often referred to as "gut feelings". Your awareness grows when you pay attention to what your gut tells you about the people, places, and events you encounter.

As your awareness grows, you can adjust your energy for different situations and activities. Your goal is not necessarily to have all your chakras fully open at all times. When you are speaking on the telephone with an angry client, you might need to close down your solar plexus chakra to keep yourself from getting angry while you open your throat chakra to increase your ability to listen attentively.

Adjusting your chakra energies is simply a matter of focusing your attention. Try imagining that each of your chakras has a volume control knob. Use your awareness to turn up or down the volume on each chakra as needed during your workday.

**CONVERSATION**
*Every conversation involves an exchange of energy. Often a person's body language, gestures, and tone convey meanings not carried by their words alone.*

**ROSE QUARTZ**
*You can improve the energy landscape of your workplace by adding flowers, plants, and crystals, such as rose quartz, which draws off negative energy and adds peaceful vibes.*

# Workday energy adjustments

Here are some other techniques you can use to adjust your energy at work.

When you are taking public transport or walking along a crowded pavement, visualize a bubble around you that protects the outer edges of your aura like a strong, flexible shield. Your aura bubble should extend in all directions – behind your back, over your head, and under your feet. Remind yourself that the bubble protects you from all negative energies, but allows positive energies to flow through to you.

Pay attention to what you experience when you sit down for a meeting at work. Notice your gut reaction to what the people are wearing, their tone of voice, facial expressions, and body language. Use your awareness to balance the energy of the group as needed: turn up the volume on your root chakra to stabilize the energy of a group that is finding it difficult to get down to business. Turn up the volume on your brow chakra when the group needs inspiration to break through to a solution.

Use the power of your voice to transform negative energy. Communication allows your energy to blend with the energy of others. In a one-on-one meeting that is getting nowhere, focus energy on your throat chakra and give voice to a question that is unspoken but hanging in the air. Doing so often shifts the conversation into a more constructive pattern.

When your energy flags during your workday, do something to change your energetic environment. Move your chair, turn on or off your desk light, put on a sweater, or take one off.

**RE-BALANCE**
*After an intense period of work at your desk, you can re-balance your energy by making yourself a relaxing cup of tea.*

# Releasing tension and stress

You already know that worry, doubt, anger, and other kinds of tension and stress can lead to problems with your physical body, including high blood pressure, heart disease, digestive disorders, and skin problems. But you may not be aware that your energy body plays a role in this process.

When the ups and downs of your workday make you feel stressed, the chakra associated with the reason for your stress reacts to the feeling. Where you experience the stress in your body is often related to the cause of

**SEATED ABDOMINAL TWIST**
*This simple exercise, which can easily be done in a chair at your desk, can help you release tension in your solar plexus area.*

*(01) Sit up straight. Place one of your hands on the area of your solar plexus chakra, just above your navel. Place the other hand on your back just above your waist. Your palms should be facing inward and facing each other.*

*(02) Take a deep breath and twist from your waist so that you are looking over your right shoulder. Don't over twist your neck. Hold your breath for several seconds.*

*(03) Exhale and return to centre. Inhale again, twisting from the waist so that you are looking over your left shoulder. Hold your breath for several seconds. Exhale and return to centre. Repeat for a total of three twists to each side.*

01

the stress. For instance, when a difficult conversation
with your boss or other authority figure makes you feel
powerless, your stomach may become upset. On an
energy level, your solar plexus chakra – related to
personal power – has registered your feeling, which is
then transmitted to nearby parts of your physical body.
Unreleased solar plexus tension can, over time, lead to
indigestion, ulcers, and other digestive problems.

   Working with your chakras helps to restore life
energy and release stress before it manifests in illness.

02                                        03

# Releasing tension in your voice

If you have difficultly speaking up at work or get nervous before you need to make a presentation, focusing energy on your throat chakra can help you release the tension and express yourself more easily. In Hindu thought, the throat chakra is shaped like a lotus flower with sixteen petals, which correspond to the sixteen vowels in the Sanskrit alphabet. So it makes sense that the throat chakra is connected to all forms of language and communication.

The easiest way to release tension in your throat is to warm up your voice. Singing in the shower or humming along with a CD or the radio as you drive to work is an excellent way to send energy to your throat chakra. Or try one of the throat chakra warm-up exercises that follow.

### USING THE BREATH TO RELAX THE VOICE

*(01) Stand or sit up straight, and close your eyes. Breathe in gently through your nose and exhale through your mouth. Repeat five times.*

*(02) Now breathe in more deeply through your nose, expanding your abdomen to allow your lungs to fill fully. Engage your voice as you exhale with a relaxed "a-a-a-h". Repeat five times.*

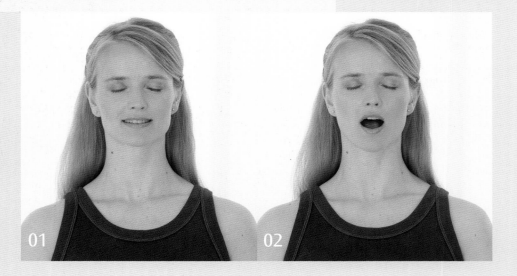

01

02

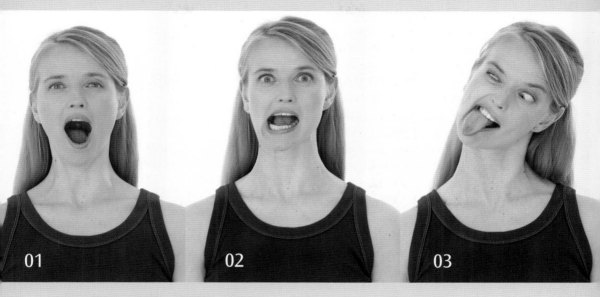

01

02

03

### RELEASING TENSION IN YOUR MOUTH AND JAW

(01) Open your mouth as wide as you can, as if you were yawning.

(02) Move your mouth, lips, tongue, and jaw into as many different positions as possible. Now, engage your voice and allow whatever sounds feel right to come out as you continue to move your mouth, tongue, and jaw.

(03) If you are lucky enough to have a private office or can use a private toilet for this exercise, try watching yourself in the mirror as you make funny faces and silly sounds. A well-functioning throat chakra improves your wit and sense of humour. Laughter helps you to relax before you need to speak.

# Accessing energy and focus

It's easy to feel enthusiasm for projects and activities that give you pleasure, like a playing a sport you enjoy or sightseeing when you're on holiday. It's often much harder to feel energetic about work tasks, especially for aspects of your job that you don't especially like or when you're feeling physically tired or hungry.

There are healthy ways and not so healthy ways to increase your energy during your workday so that you can focus on what needs to be done. Not so healthy ways include reaching for an external stimulant, like another cup of coffee or piece of chocolate. Though caffeine and sugar do stimulate your energy levels temporarily, their effects wear off quickly. Over time, the use of external energy stimulants depletes your body and makes it harder for you to access energy and focus from healthy, internal sources.

The first step in managing your energy in a healthy way is increasing your awareness of your own patterns. Pay attention as you work to changes in your level of energy and enthusiasm. Do you find it harder to focus at a particular time of day? Is it difficult to feel energetic about a particular aspect of your job or about interacting with a particular person? Do you experience a drop in your energy when certain thoughts or feelings come up during your workday, such as worries about your childcare arrangements?

Also pay attention to times and activities that naturally boost your energy. Is it easier to focus after an early lunch and a brisk walk? Do you find it easier to feel enthusiastic about certain parts of your job, perhaps tasks that make you feel particularly

**INSTANT ENERGY BOOSTS**

■ *A bright red apple strengthens the energy of the root chakra and helps you stay grounded.*

■ *The vibrant orange of tangerines and raw carrots strengthens your sacral chakra and helps you go with the flow.*

■ *A sunny yellow banana soothes and strengthens your solar plexus chakra for increased power and vitality.*

■ *Green apples and celery sticks open and balance your heart chakra for improved empathy and compassion.*

■ *Blueberries are the perfect snack to strengthen your throat chakra and improve your ability to communicate.*

■ *Purple grapes and plums enhance the energy of your brow and crown chakras, improving your access to intuition and creative imagination.*

competent or those that require that you collaborate
with others, rather than work on your own?

Awareness of your own patterns can help you make
changes in your workday routine to keep your body
nourished and your energies humming.

### RAW FOOD SNACKS

Your body requires a variety of fresh foods to maintain
health and energy. Eating raw fruits and vegetables is
especially important to maintaining your energy body
in peak condition. Keep a supply of raw food snacks
at work. Choose colourful fruits and vegetables that
complement and strengthen the vibration of each
chakra. Eating raw foods rather than crisps, biscuits,
or chocolate nourishes both your physical body and
your energy body.

# Special focus: the solar plexus chakra

The Sanskrit name for the solar plexus chakra is *manipura*, which means "lustrous gem". Radiating golden yellow fire energy, the third chakra lights the body from the inside with warmth, solar energy, and personal power.

When your solar plexus chakra is functioning well, it is a limitless internal source of vitality, drive, and passion. It can inspire you to take responsibility for creating your own life by helping you realize who you are at your very core, and by providing the motivation for you to take the necessary steps to realize your full potential.

To get ahead in your career and in life, you need a clear vision of what you want to accomplish. The ability to envision is related to the functioning of the brow chakra (see pages 128–129). However, no matter how clear your goals, you also need the motivation and will to do what's needed to manifest your dreams. A strong solar plexus chakra helps you to combine your power, ambition, drive, and sense of purpose to create the prosperous career and the abundant life you want.

An imbalance in your solar plexus chakra can lead to feelings of helplessness or victimization. You may feel perpetually stressed out and irritable, or be unable to get over feelings of anger, bitterness, jealousy, or resentment. You may have a tendency to blame others when things go wrong. Alternately, a poorly functioning third chakra can manifest in the desire to be in control, to tell others what to do and how to act. Ironically, both feeling powerless and feeling a strong need to dominate others often arise from the same source – a damaged sense of your own self-worth.

Bringing consciousness to your body's power centre at the solar plexus can help you to resolve these problems and move ahead with energy and purpose toward reaching your goals.

## METHODS FOR STRENGTHENING YOUR SOLAR PLEXUS CHAKRA

| Where to focus | What to do |
| --- | --- |
| Foods | Eat complex carbohydrates, such as bananas, whole grains, and brown rice. |
| Colour therapy | Get up early enough to watch the sunrise; take walks in the sunshine; put a vase of daffodils on your desk. |
| Aromatherapy | Put a few drops of juniper, geranium, or vertiver in the water bowl of an oil burner warmed by a tea-light candle. |
| Crystals | Wear gold or amber jewellery at your wrist or throat. |
| Clothes | Wear a gold-coloured blouse or shirt or wrap a belt with a gold buckle around your waist. |
| Self-care | Replace external stimulants such as coffee, caffeine, and sugar with healthy snacks, including raw fruits and vegetables. |
| Recreation | Engage in an active sport, something that gets you running. |
| House and home | Let go of something you are holding on to that you no longer need; clean out the cellar; give away old clothes. |
| Journal exercise | Write about: when do I feel most powerful? When do I feel least powerful? What are my career/life goals? What steps do I need to take to manifest them? |

01

### INNER SUN MEDITATION

*Many ancient cultures regarded the sun as the centre of the universe or worshipped it as a powerful god. Meditating on your inner sun fills your personal universe with powerful life-force energy.*

*(01) Sit comfortably with a straight back on a cushion on the floor or in a chair. Close your eyes. Breathe slowly and deeply. With each inhalation, become more aware of the solar plexus chakra located between your navel and the bottom of your breastbone.*

*(02) As you breathe in, imagine that this chakra is made of golden yellow light, shining like an inner sun. With each inhalation, feel that your breath is causing this inner sun to radiate more and more brilliant yellow light.*

*(03) As you breathe out, imagine that the warming and invigorating energy of this inner sun is spreading throughout your body, from your toes to the top of your head, filling you with energy, vitality, power, and focus.*

# Challenging your thoughts

You are probably aware that you are always talking to yourself inside your head. This continuous inner dialogue consists largely of commentary about your life – memories, feelings, thoughts about people and events, and plans for the future.

The words and ideas that run through your mind have an enormous impact. Like an old song you can't get out of your head, they play constantly, colouring your reactions to what's happening to you right now. For instance, if your inner voice whispers, "My boss doesn't appreciate me. I'll never get ahead in this job", you probably won't – not because your negative thoughts have caused this result, but because they lead you to sabotage your personal power from within. When your boss comes around, instead of showing off your best self, you are irritable, defensive, and blaming. Naturally, when an opportunity for advancement comes up, your boss looks elsewhere. Affirmations give you the chance to replace these old songs with more positive ideas and concepts.

**AFFIRMATIONS**
*Affirmations linked to the solar plexus chakra help you let go of anger, bitterness, and resentment and claim your personal power, drive, and sense of purpose.*

*1. Read through these sample solar plexus affirmations:*
■ *I am self-assertive in my dealings with others.*
■ *I can say "yes" or "no" according to what I really feel.*
■ *I claim my authentic power.*

*2. Now write five solar plexus affirmations of your own.*

*3. Find some creative ways to remind yourself of these positive statements. For example:*
■ *Write each affirmation on an index card and decorate them with colourful designs.*
■ *Draw a card each morning to be your "keyword" for the day ahead.*
■ *Use them as screen savers on your computer.*

# Special focus: the throat chakra

The Sanskrit name for the throat chakra is *visuddha*, which means "purification". The throat is the narrow passageway between the body and the mind. As the name of this chakra implies, physical matter needs to be purified before it can ascend into the realm of the spiritual, governed by the brow and crown chakras.

In addition to interpersonal communication, the throat chakra also helps you to communicate with yourself. Without it, you could not interpret the signals you get from your body or regulate the chatter going on in your mind. A well-functioning throat chakra also improves your personal creativity – your ability to express yourself through writing, music, dance, and the visual arts.

A poorly functioning throat chakra makes it very difficult for you to speak up when you need to, or to communicate in writing with clarity and power. It may also make it difficult for you to understand what other people are telling you, or you may misinterpret their nonverbal signals, leading to problems at work and in your personal relationships.

## SEED SYLLABLES

In Hindu thought, all sound is sacred. Each sound is in essence an energy pattern that brings you into resonance with the thing that is named. Each chakra has its own associated sound – its "seed syllable" – a sound that expresses its vibratory energy.

Use the power of your throat chakra to balance the energy of all seven chakras before you begin your workday. Starting at the base of your spine with the

| SEED SYLLABLES | |
|---|---|
| **Chakra** | **Sound** |
| Root | LAM |
| Sacral | VAM |
| Solar plexus | RAM |
| Heart | YAM |
| Throat | HAM |
| Brow | OM |
| Crown | silence |

root chakra, focus your attention on each chakra as
you pronounce or chant its seed syllable, allowing the
final "m" to vibrate powerfully as "mmmmmm".

| METHODS FOR STRENGTHENING YOUR THROAT CHAKRA | |
| --- | --- |
| *Where to focus* | *What to do* |
| Foods | Eat all kinds of fruit, including blueberries and grapes. |
| Colour therapy | Visualize that with each slow and gentle breath your throat is being bathed with soothing blue light. |
| Aromatherapy | Drink chamomile tea; place a few drops of lavender oil at the base of your neck. |
| Crystals | Wear a turquoise necklace; carry a piece of tumbled blue lace agate or sodalite. |
| Clothes | Wear a sweater with a beautiful high collar or decorative neckline; tie a bright blue scarf around your neck. |
| Self-care | Visit the dentist; buy new lipstick or gloss; be sure to laugh out loud at least once a day. |
| Recreation | Join a choir or singing group; attend a musical play, symphony concert or opera; read poetry aloud; listen to all kinds of music. |
| House and home | Clean and organize your bookshelves and music collection; catch up on emails; send someone a birthday card or thank you note. |
| Journaling exercise | Write a letter you will never mail to someone with whom you have unfinished communication, like an ex-boss, former lover, or even someone who is no longer living. |

# Finding your authentic voice

All too often, speaking up at work means saying what you think you should so that others will like you, or saying what you think others want to hear. Finding your authentic voice means giving yourself permission to say what you truly think and feel in a way that is skillful, compassionate, and respectful of yourself and others.

Here are some ways you can use the energy of your throat chakra to find and free your authentic voice:

### Journaling your inner voice
Set aside ten minutes each evening to write in your journal or notebook the things you felt or thought but found it difficult to say aloud during the course of the day. Also write about times during the day (or in your life) when you felt really listened to and times when someone "shuts you down by not listening".

**HAVING YOUR SAY**
*Use your journal to practise having your say. Write both what you said when someone criticized you and what you didn't say.*

### Rehearsal

If you are having trouble finding the right words to say to someone, place a picture of the person or an object that reminds you of what you wish to say in a place where you will see it every day. Whenever you look at the picture or object, take a moment to speak to the person in your mind, rehearsing what you want to say until it feels clear, kind, and authentic.

### Communicating with compassion

Pay attention to the tone, intensity, and emotional impact of your words and written communications. For instance, a woman whose job it was to write rejection letters trained herself to add one positive comment to each letter to soften its impact. Doing so made her feel better about her job and about herself.

**PHOTO REHEARSAL**
*After practising a private conversation with the person's photo, find a good time to say aloud what you have rehearsed.*

# CHAPTER FOUR

# Chakras and your relationships

In many ways, the quality of your relationships determines the quality of your life. A strong and mutually supportive connection to your family, friends, colleagues – in fact, to all people everywhere including yourself – brings you joy and happiness and gives meaning and direction to your life.

The two chakras most closely linked to your ability to relate well to others are the sacral chakra and the heart chakra. Building on the security and self-esteem of the root chakra, the sacral chakra encourages you to reach out to others to give and receive emotional support. A well-functioning sacral chakra connects you to your feelings and gives you a sense of natural flexibility, flow, and balance. When it's appropriate, the sacral chakra also fuels your desire to reach out to others for touch, intimacy, and sensual pleasure.

The heart chakra adds the bonds of love to your relationships. Love can be personal and focused on a particular person, or it can be universal, a feeling of compassion and empathy that spreads outward from the heart to all people everywhere. Love helps you to accept and respect the people you love as they are, to see the good in everyone, and to forgive others and yourself. As you open your heart chakra, your spirit expands to help you meet the opportunities and challenges of your life with optimism and acceptance.

In this chapter, you'll find suggestions and exercises that can help you improve the quality and depth of your relationships. As you'll discover, loving and accepting yourself exactly as you are right now is the essential basis for developing fulfilling relationships with others.

# The dance of emotions

For some people, private feelings are mysterious and dangerous. They fear that "giving in" to their feelings or expressing them too strongly will cause them to lose control or make them vulnerable to being hurt. They often hide their feelings and feel uncomfortable when strong emotions are on display.

Other people love the sensation of swimming in the sea of strong feelings. They believe that emotions of all kinds – both pleasurable and painful – make life worth living. They often lead with their emotions – *feeling* something to be important or true before they *know* it. People who enjoy emotions are seldom shy about letting others know how they feel.

Take a moment to ask yourself where you fall on this emotional scale. If you are a person who finds the easy flow of emotions to be a challenge, working with the energies of your chakras can help you learn to dance

***EBB AND FLOW***
*Your emotional energy has a natural ebb and flow, and often alternates between times of low intensity, and times when you experience powerfully deep feelings.*

more easily and playfully with your feelings, and the thoughts they come from, throughout your busy day.

At the level of the sacral chakra, emotions are relatively simple. Your most basic emotions are desire ("I want that") and hatred ("I don't want that"). By wanting things you are motivated to make choices and take appropriate action.

Hatred motivates you to push things away, especially things that cause you unhappiness or pain. At the level of the sacral chakra, hatred motivates you to defend yourself from attack by fighting back or by running away. However, being overly defensive can cause you to shut down emotionally and to deny yourself joyful feelings because you fear experiencing painful ones. Ideally, your goal should be to dance gracefully within the push and pull of emotions without shutting down or losing your balance.

**DESIRE**
*Desire pulls you toward the things you want to experience or possess — everything from a better job or the ideal partner, to another piece of chocolate cake.*

### DANCING YOUR FEELINGS

*Try this exercise on a weekend or after work as a way to unwind. Though you might feel self-conscious at first about dancing alone, allowing your body to move freely to music is an excellent way for you to release tension and get in touch with your feelings. All physical movement, but especially dance, stimulates the free flow of the body's energy and connects you with the pleasure of relating emotionally to all those people you come in contact with.*

*Depending on the music you choose, your dance can be gentle and meditative or sensual and wild. You can also dance through a whole range of emotions by changing the music and varying your movements. When you finish your dance, write about anything memorable you experienced in your journal.*

*(01) Clear a space where you can move freely. Make sure that you are wearing loose clothing. Take off your shoes. Put on music that mirrors your current feeling about someone in your life or expresses a range of feelings you would like to experience. Before you start to dance, stand still and in the present for a few minutes and let the music move through your feet, legs, and belly.*

01

(02) Start to move in any way that feels right. Let your body lead you without holding back. Your dance may include any movement or series of movements in any style. Keep your attention focused on your body. Don't think about what you are doing or allow feelings of embarrassment to hold you back.

(03) Don't be surprised if dancing intensifies your feelings or brings up memories and emotions that are hiding below the surface of consciousness. Emotions are stored not only in your brain but also in the bones, muscles, and organs influenced by each chakra. Moving your hips, for instance, may allow sexual feelings and memories to rise into consciousness. Moving your arms and shoulders in a way that expands your chest may stimulate the free flow of loving feelings. Allow whatever memories and feelings arise to become part of your dance. Continue dancing until it feels right to stop.

# Setting boundaries

An important part of experiencing the free flow of emotions is setting boundaries. Just as damaging as shutting down your feelings is opening them too widely or without proper discrimination. When your emotions are allowed total free play, you may find yourself swinging back and forth between elation and depression, rather than letting your feelings flow in a gentle and natural rhythm.

Similarly, when your emotional connections to other people are too extreme, you may be too easily influenced by what other people are feeling – catching their anger and excitement rather than honouring your own responses.

## CHAKRA ENERGIZING TECHNIQUES
Listed here are some chakra energy techniques you can use to set appropriate emotional boundaries.
- Carnelian and tiger's eye are helpful crystals for stabilizing emotions and moods. Wearing a carnelian pendant calms your anger and offers protection against other people's envy and resentment. Its orange-red colour stimulates the sacral chakra and encourages the free flow of sexual feelings. Carrying a piece of tiger's eye is another powerful talisman against the negative emotions of others. Tiger's eye also stabilizes your feelings and balances the energies of your lower chakras.
- On days when you are feeling emotionally vulnerable, pull your aura more tightly around you for a feeling of safety. Close your eyes and visualize that your aura is a rainbow-coloured cloak or shawl.

### CRYSTAL PENDANT
*Wearing a pendant with an orange-red crystal, such as carnelian or amber, balances your emotions by stimulating energy flow to each of your lower chakras.*

Imagine that you are wrapping this colourful cloak more tightly around your body so that you are completely protected. Be sure to allow this tightness to relax when you are feeling more at ease.

■ The Sanskrit word *mantra* means "mind protection". You can devise your own mantras to help you set appropriate boundaries. Repeating "I love and appreciate myself just as I am" under your breath strengthens your heart chakra to protect you from being hurt by criticism. "I can go with the flow" strengthens your sacral chakra so that you can get along with difficult people without shutting down.

# Awakening your heart

The most profound and life changing emotions are love and compassion, both of which arise from the free flow of life energy through the heart chakra. In Buddhist philosophy, love is the wish for others to be happy. Compassion – literally "suffering with" – is the wish for others to be free from everything that might cause them suffering.

In essence, love and compassion are two sides of the same coin. To love another person is to want more than anything for that person to be completely and permanently happy. You are able to separate people you truly love from their behaviour and love them unconditionally, even when you dislike what they do. Isn't that exactly how a parent feels about a child, or a lover feels about a beloved?

Because love is such a powerful emotion, you experience it in stages. Not surprisingly, these stages mirror your chakras.

■ At the level of your root chakra, the drive for survival and stability teaches you basic self-love, the feeling that you cherish yourself enough to keep yourself safe.

■ At the sacral chakra level, self-love expands to include other people, with whom you share the desire to care and be cared for, to nurture and be nurtured. Here, too, the desire for touch and sensual pleasure brings you into intimate connection with others.

■ At the solar plexus, your view of love expands further to include love for external goals – a fulfilling career, a comfortable home, and an abundant life.

■ Awakening your heart at the level of the fourth chakra infuses love with spirit. The feeling of being

**COMMITMENT**
*Successful marriages and other loving partnerships each require an energy commitment from all of the chakras.*

in love illuminates the person you love and everything else with a magical or spiritual glow. As your heart chakras bond, the boundaries between you and the loved person dissolve, and you experience the joy of empathy, respect, and complete acceptance.

■ At the level of the three higher chakras, the throat, the brow, and the crown, the spiritual aspect of love expands even further. Your love spreads beyond your own life and concerns out into the universe to embrace everything that exists in a blissful union of harmony and peace.

***UNCONDITIONAL LOVE***
*Ideally, a parent's love for their child is unconditional, and not based on approval or disapproval of the child's behaviour.*

# Opening your heart to love

Awakening your heart chakra deepens and intensifies all of your relationships. It helps you to accept the conditions and people in your life – your partner, kids, mother-in-law, chatty neighbour, and grumpy boss – exactly as they are right now. Lovingly accepting and forgiving others, including people who may have hurt you deeply, releases life energy that may have been stuck for years. This energy boost increases your ability to enjoy and appreciate life.

Here is a meditation you can use at any time, lying down or sitting, to awaken and open your heart chakra.

**THE ROSE**

*1. Sit comfortably or lie on your back on a yoga mat or blanket.*

*2. Spend a few minutes watching your breath, paying attention to the expansion and contraction of your chest as you breathe. Listen to the sound of your heartbeat.*

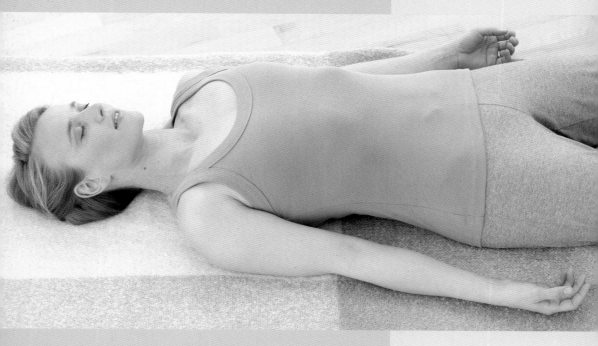

3. Bring to mind the image of someone you love or have loved strongly in your life. Remember their face, way of walking and speaking, the clothes they wear, their favourite activities and foods. Put yourself into the scene and remember how it is to spend time with them, paying special attention to your feelings. Appreciate as fully as you can everything that is wonderful about this relationship.

4. Now turn your attention to your heart chakra. Visualize it as a beautiful budding rose. Allow the warm feelings you have for the loved person you are remembering to open up the petals of the rosebud gently and slowly until your heart rose is in full and glorious bloom.

5. Allow the love streaming from your open heart to touch everyone you care for with your wish for them to be complete and happy.

**THE ROSE**
In yoga texts, the heart chakra is imaged as a lotus, but in many contemporary cultures, the flower most often associated with the heart is the rose.

# Special focus: the sacral chakra

In Sanskrit, the second chakra is called *svadhisthana*, which means "sweetness". The name reminds you of the sweet delights of desire, touch, and sexual pleasure. The element associated with this chakra is water. When you experience physical pleasure, whether from a relaxing backrub, the joy of dance or movement, or the embrace of someone you love, your sensations and feelings flow like water.

Work with the second chakra is aimed at helping to encourage the free flow of your emotions. If you have been hurt in your relationships, you may have closed down this flow to keep from being hurt again. Opening to past memories is sometimes painful, but it is a necessary first step to getting your emotional energy moving again. Reaching out to a trusted friend with whom you can share your feelings or consulting a therapist can be helpful to this process. You might also try expressing your painful feelings creatively, through journaling, drawing, or painting, since the sacral chakra is also the source of creative and artistic ideas.

It is also possible to react to past hurts by becoming overly emotional. When the energy of the sacral chakra is excessive, you may crave the stimulation of intense feelings. Your life becomes a whirl of too many partners and too many parties. Balancing the energy of the second chakra can help resolve this problem as well. The goal is a more gentle emotional rhythm – a proper balance of time with others and time alone, of social events and quiet evenings at home.

Sexuality is also an expression of the energy of the sacral chakra. Blockages of second chakra energy can make it difficult for you to feel desire or experience sexual pleasure. A well-functioning second chakra opens you to the joys of tenderness – of touching and being touched, giving and receiving.

## METHODS FOR STRENGTHENING YOUR SACRAL CHAKRA

| Where to focus | What to do |
|---|---|
| Foods | Drink plenty of liquids, especially water. |
| Colour therapy | Place a bowl of juicy oranges or tangerines on your kitchen counter or dining table. |
| Aromatherapy | Wear a few drops of jasmine, sandalwood, or ylang ylang perfume to stimulate your sensuality. |
| Crystals | Place orange-red fire opal on your sacral chakra to support you through emotional difficulties. |
| Clothes | Wear a blouse or scarf made of silk, chiffon or other flowing fabric; buy some new lingerie that makes you feel sexy. |
| Self-care | Get a massage; soak in a hot tub; light candles and take a long, sensuous, bubble bath. |
| Recreation | Sign up for dance lessons with a partner or by yourself; watch a sexy movie; explore something new in your lovemaking. |
| House and home | Add a fountain, aquarium, pond, or other water feature to your home or garden. |
| Journal exercise | Write about: what emotion did I feel most strongly today? How did this feeling affect my thoughts and actions? |

# Partner chakra massage

Massage can be relaxing and soothing – it can also be sensual and erotic. This energizing chakra massage can be enjoyed for its own sake, but it is also a wonderful warm-up for lovemaking. Take turns with your partner giving and receiving so that both partners can enjoy the pleasure of sensuous touch.

Find a private and intimate space that you can use. Be sure the room is warm enough for you to be comfortable without clothes, and check that there is a comfortable mattress or bed and pillows to use. Select a warming massage oil that contains jasmine, sandalwood, patchouli, bergamot, or clary sage. Protect your bed linen with fluffy towels.

**WARMING OIL**
*Use plenty of massage oil to encourage a deep, releasing, and enjoyable massage.*

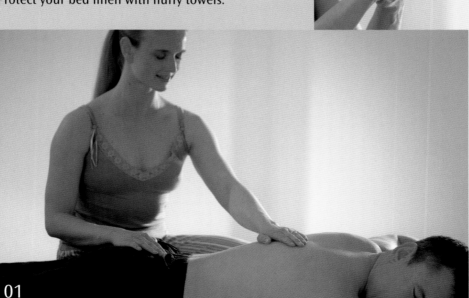

01

## ENERGIZING CHAKRA MASSAGE

*(01) Ask your partner to lie facedown on the bed. Make him comfortable by placing a pillow under his upper chest. Place your right hand on your partner's lower back at the sacrum, just below the spine. Place your left hand at the middle of your partner's back, directly behind the heart chakra. Close your eyes and tune in to the rhythm of your partner's breathing, synchronizing it with your own for several minutes.*

*(02) Begin to massage the base of your partner's spine to energize the sacral chakra, using small circular movements. Place one hand on top of the other, if you wish.*

2

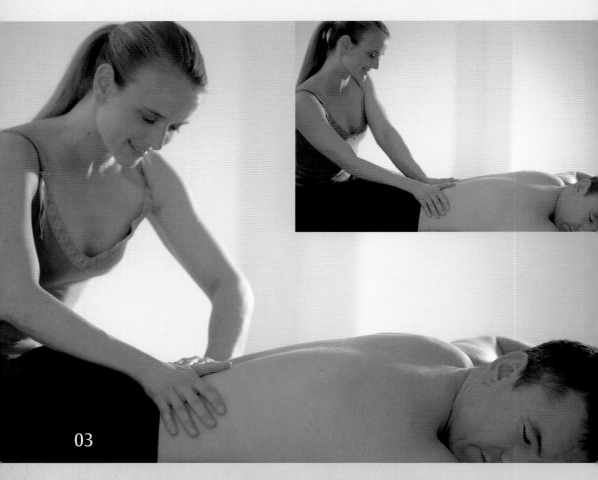

03

*(03) After a few moments, move your hands up your partner's spine to massage the area behind the naval to energize the solar plexus chakra. Massage either side of the spine, not directly on it.*

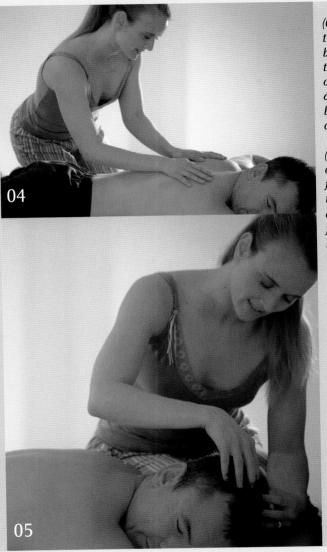

(04) Moving upward, massage the middle of your partner's back for the heart chakra, the shoulders and the back of the neck for the throat chakra, and then, for the brow chakra, the back of the head.

(05) When you reach the top of the head, use only your fingertips and a very light touch to energize the crown chakra. When your massage feels complete, reverse roles so that your partner can use the same technique on you.

# Special focus: the heart chakra

The heart chakra is the central point of your energy body. Below are the three "material" chakras, which focus on meeting your needs for physical security, sexual expression, and worldly power and will. Above are the three "spiritual" chakras, which focus on the communication and expression of your essential spirit.

In Sanskrit, the heart chakra is called *anahata*, which means "the sound that is made without any two things striking". The name refers to the harmonious feeling you get when you are no longer fighting (or striking out) to achieve what you want but rather relaxing into loving union with it. This loving union expands your spirit so that you can embrace others with compassion, respect, and acceptance.

Loving yourself is an essential prerequisite to entering into a loving union with someone else. Unless you forgive and accept yourself and view your own failings – everything you do that is childish, selfish, silly, or hurtful – with compassion, you'll find it difficult to believe that anyone else could find you loveable.

A lack of self-love affects the heart chakra in one of two ways. Either the heart chakra closes down, which causes you to avoid intimate connections with others. You may feel depressed or ashamed, or you might armour your heart and dismiss all loving feelings as fairy tale fantasies. Or, the heart chakra opens too wide, without appropriate boundaries. You may enter into relationships in which you sacrifice your own needs and rely on another person to make you feel happy and whole. Rather than bringing you joy and satisfaction, such relationships generally bring the suffering of instability, fear, control, and anger.

When heart chakra energy is directed inward and honoured, you are able both to love yourself and to direct loving feelings toward others.

## METHODS FOR STRENGTHENING YOUR HEART CHAKRA

| Where to focus | What to do |
| --- | --- |
| Foods | Eat plenty of vegetables, especially greens. |
| Colour therapy | Buy yourself or someone you love a dozen red roses to celebrate a relationship anniversary. |
| Aromatherapy | Use lotions, skin creams, and bath oils containing rose essential oils, such as rose absolute and rose otto. |
| Crystals | Place a rose quartz crystal under your pillow or next to your bed to open your heart and invite love into your life. |
| Clothes | Wear something emerald green close to your heart. |
| Self-care | Increase self-love by taking the first step toward ending an unhealthy addiction, such as to food, cigarettes, or coffee. |
| Recreation | Make the time to reconnect with friends and family – have a party; meet a friend for tea; plan a weekend getaway with your partner or close friend. |
| House and home | Make sure the air in your home is fresh and circulating properly; hang a wind chime in your garden. |
| Journaling exercise | Write about: the things I appreciate most about my partner, friend, mother/father or sister/brother; why it's sometimes hard for me to love myself. |

### REDISCOVERING ROMANCE

*If a formerly loving relationship has grown stale, this heart chakra exercise can help you and your partner fall in love all over again.*

*1. Sit opposite your partner. Look into each other's eyes. First, help each other remember the little things you used to do to show your love. Taking turns, each partner shares a memory from the most romantic time in the relationship. Begin each memory with the phrase, "I used to feel so loved and cared for when you …" For instance: wrote me love letters; sent me flowers; walked with me to the train every morning; took off my shoes and rubbed my feet; called me from work just to say hello.*

*2. After about five minutes, or when the first part seems complete, share with your partner the little things you appreciate most about your current relationship. Taking turns, each partner completes the phrase, "I appreciate when you …" For instance: remember to call me when you're going to be late; sit next to me when we're watching TV; compliment me on how I look; cook my favourite dinner; listen to me when I'm upset.*

*3. After about five minutes, or when this part seems complete, share with your partner the little things you've always wanted but have never asked for. These can include private fantasies. Begin each request with the phrase, "I would feel so loved and cared for if you would …" For instance: give me a kiss and a hug when you come home from work; shampoo my hair; buy me something sexy as a surprise present; spend the night with me at a hotel; massage me for thirty minutes.*

*4. Try to fulfil one of your partner's requests each week. Acknowledge with appreciation the loving things your partner does. Don't keep score! Regard each thing you do as a love gift, which is presented freely with an open heart without the expectation that it will be reciprocated.*

# The breath of love

The heart chakra's element is air. Breathing into your partner's heart chakra as he breathes into yours is a powerful way to deepen your love relationship. It can help partners who are in a tough place restore their intimate heart connection.

Find a private and intimate space and make sure the room is warm enough for you to be comfortable without clothes. Arrange candles, flowers, soft music, and a comfortable and supportive pillow for each partner to sit on. If you wish, light a stick of incense or put a few drops of rose, lavender, or jasmine oil in the water bowl of an oil burner.

**PARTNER BREATHING**
*(01) Sit back-to-back with your partner, both of you sitting on a pillow. Gently lean against each other so your root, sacral, and heart chakras are touching. As you breathe in, visualize that the inhaled air coming in through your nose travels down your spine, exits your body at your heart chakra, and enters your partner's body at the heart chakra. Your partner should do the same visualization.*

*(02) Continue this for at least five minutes, feeling your heart relax and open to the breath of love as you send this breath of love to your partner. When your visualization seems complete, squeeze your partner's hand to signal an ending.*

*(03) Close with a warm and tender mutual embrace.*

**ROSE IN BLOOM**
*Breathing into each other's heart chakras helps to release constrictions so that each heart can open like a rose coming into full bloom.*

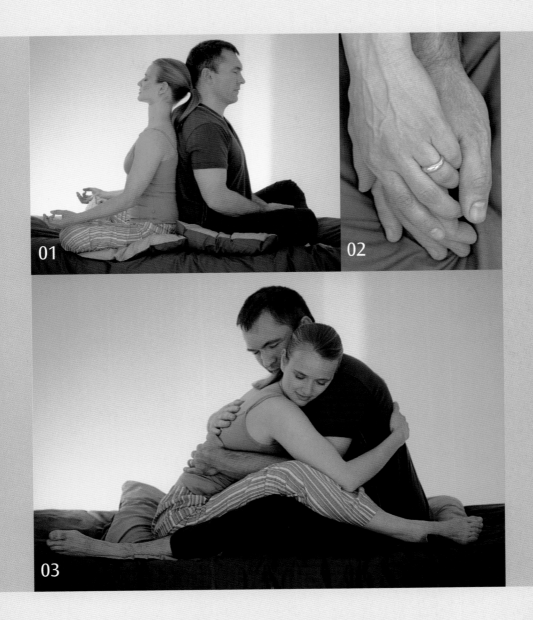

CHAPTER FIVE

# Chakra healing

By now you know that your chakras influence many

aspects of your life. As you are discovering, each

chakra oversees a different set of emotional and

psychological concerns. And working with your

chakras can also help you improve your health.

As you will learn in this chapter, when you are ill or have a health problem, it usually indicates that the chakra corresponding to some part of your body is out of balance. Conversely, when your life energy is flowing smoothly, you are more likely to have a healthy life, even if that life happens to include an illness.

Healing your body and mind by working on your chakras is not a substitute for traditional medical care, however, it can help in several practical ways. For one thing, popular complementary therapies, including colour healing, sound healing, and crystal therapy, focus on strengthening and balancing your chakra energies. You'll learn some basic techniques for integrating these therapies into your busy day in this chapter. Moreover, a deeper understanding of the energetic forces related to your health problems accelerates your healing by helping you make better decisions about treatment plans and lifestyle issues.

Physical symptoms and diseases are generally the last place that an energetic imbalance shows up. Illness is often a way that your body calls your attention to a life issue you have ignored for too long. Thus by balancing and strengthening your chakras, you both improve your current health and also take preventive measures that can help you stay healthy in the future.

# Energy medicine

Working with your body's energy is an accessible and safe form of healing. Contemporary energy healing combines scientific knowledge of the body with an intuitive understanding of the flow of body energy. While professional energy healers are an important resource, learning to work with your own energy empowers you to take greater responsibility for your health by providing you with do-it-yourself healing methods that are simple, comforting, and natural.

As you work with your chakra energies following the suggestions in this book, your ability to choose appropriate therapies will improve naturally. Here is a good way to get started:

If you are suffering from a particular illness or health condition, locate it on the chart on page 101.

**SOUND ENERGY**
*Though energy medicine feels very modern, the practice is actually very old. The sound of drums, gongs, and singing bowls has been used in many cultures to tune and heal the energy body.*

Reread the special focus section on the chakra related to this condition and then think carefully about the psychological and emotional concerns and lifestyle issues that may be related to your problem. Making improvements in these areas of your life may relieve your condition, or at least, make it easier for you to cope with it.

For instance, if your health problem is frequently catching chest colds, coughs, and bronchitis, think about issues related to the heart chakra. Ask yourself: Am I loving and compassionate to myself? Is there anyone in my life I have been unable to forgive? Is there any loss I have not taken time to grieve? Exploring these issues in your journal can be the first step toward resolving your health problem.

**COLOURED SAND**
*Native American shamans used coloured sand in their healing rituals. Tibetan Buddhist sand mandalas like this one are still used as aids to meditation and inner healing.*

# Chakras and your health

This chart shows the parts of the body influenced by each chakra and the potential health consequences of energy imbalances in that chakra. Keep in mind that the chakras influence the body through subtle tendencies and potentials, and that energy imbalances do not cause the health problems listed here. However, you'll find this chart useful in deciding which of the therapies in this chapter can help you the most.

**POINTS OF VIEW**
*Health problems are often related to a combination of physical, emotional, and energetic factors. Healing can be accelerated when you explore all of these points of view.*

| CHAKRA | BODY PARTS | POTENTIAL HEALTH PROBLEMS |
|---|---|---|
| Root | Pelvis, legs, ankles, feet, hips, rectum, immune system | Sciatica, varicose veins, pelvic pain, rectal tumours, haemorrhoids, problems with hips, knees, ankles, feet |
| Sacral | Sexual organs, large intestine, kidney, bladder, appendix, lower spine | Lower back pain, gynaecological problems, pre-menstrual tension, infertility, impotence, prostate cancer, bladder infections, appendicitis, kidney stones |
| Solar plexus | Stomach, liver, spleen, gallbladder, pancreas, small intestines, middle spine | Ulcers, colon cancer, diabetes, indigestion, eating disorders, hepatitis, gallstones, constipation, diarrhoea |
| Heart | Heart and circulatory system, ribs, chest, lungs, shoulders, arms, breasts, upper spine | High blood pressure, heart disease, bronchitis, asthma, pneumonia, shoulder problems, breast cancer |
| Throat | Throat, neck, mouth, teeth, gums, jaw, thyroid, neck vertebrae, oesophagus | Sore throat, laryngitis, frequent colds, gum disease, dental problems, thyroid problems, swollen glands, stiff neck |
| Brow | Brain, central nervous system, eyes, ears, nose, sinuses, pituitary gland, pineal gland | Epilepsy, eye problems, sinus infection, headaches, migraine, stroke, deafness, insomnia, nightmares |
| Crown | Conditions affecting whole body systems: skeletal system, muscular system, skin, neurological system | Chronic exhaustion not linked to a physical disease, skin diseases, environmental illness, neurosis, mental illness |

# Healing with colour

As you have learned, each of the seven chakra vibrates at a wavelength that corresponds to one of the seven rainbow colours. The colours are listed on pages 20–21. If you could see your chakras as some energy healers do, they would appear as rotating wheels of coloured light, perhaps 8–13 cm (3–5 in) in diameter. In a healthy body, the chakras are aligned vertically, and all are about the same size. Each chakra also displays its own clear, distinct, and characteristic colour.

Though you may not be able to see your chakras with your physical eyes, you can use your mind to sense them. If you wake up one morning feeling unwell, take a moment to look inside and see what you can sense

01

**CHAKRA COLOUR HEALING**
*(01) Close your eyes and visualize the colour that corresponds to the chakra you wish to strengthen.*

*(02) Place your hands over your eyes and visualize that the colour is flowing into your hands, charging them with colour energy.*

*(03) Place both hands over the chakra you wish to strengthen and visualize that the colour is pouring from your hands into the chakra, balancing and strengthening its energy.*

about your chakras. Gently focus your attention on each chakra in turn, starting with the root chakra. Ask yourself, what do I sense about the size, alignment, and colour of this chakra? Move your attention up your body, chakra by chakra, trusting your intuition to alert you to any problems.

If you sense a variation in the colour of one of your chakras – for instance, a throat chakra that is pastel rather than vivid blue, or a heart chakra that is dark and muddy rather than bright green – use the colour healing technique below to balance and strengthen its energy. Colour can also be eaten as food, worn as clothing, or enjoyed as a floral bouquet.

02          03

# Sound healing

You already know that sound has a powerful effect on your mind and body. Slow tempo music can slow your breathing rate and metabolism, while listening to up-tempo rhythms can get your blood pumping. Music also affects your emotions. Listening to harmonious music can trigger the release of pleasure hormones, reduce pain, and calm your nervous system.

Given what you know about the chakras, you can easily understand how sound healing works at the energetic level. Sound is an energy wave that causes

**TIBETAN SINGING BOWL**
*Tibetan singing bowls are made of metal alloys. They come with a wooden mallet or striker. Before you buy a singing bowl, experiment with several to find one that sounds harmonious to you. Or, look for a bowl that is "tuned" to resonate with a particular chakra note. As the bowl sings during this exercise, remind yourself that your chakras are vibrating in harmony with the soothing and relaxing sounds.*

*(01) To play a singing bowl, hold it in the palm of your hand so that the bowl can vibrate freely. Tap the bowl with the wooden stick to begin the vibration.*

*(02) Then rub the outside rim of the bowl with the stick, keeping an even pressure.*

*(03) The pitch of the bowl depends on its thickness, size and weight. You can control the tone and volume by varying the location and force the tap and the speed of your rubbing.*

01

air molecules to vibrate at a particular speed. On the musical scale, high notes vibrate more quickly than low notes. As you might expect, each of the seven chakra is associated with one of the muscical notes.

The simplest way to heal your chakras with sound is to listen to beautiful music. Get comfortable, close your eyes, and remind yourself as you listen that the musical notes are resonating with and tuning your chakras. You can also try this exercise, which uses a Tibetan singing bowl.

## CHAKRAS AND MUSIC

| Chakra | Musical Note |
|---|---|
| Root | C |
| Sacral | D |
| Solar plexus | E |
| Heart | F |
| Throat | G |
| Brow | A |
| Crown | B |

# Crystal healing

One of the best ways to heal your chakras is with crystals. Crystals are superb energy transmitters. Whether you wear them as jewellery, carry them in your pocket, use them to decorate your home or office, or place them directly on your chakra points as in the exercise on pages 110–11, they work powerfully to open your energy pathways, dissolve blockages, and balance your energy.

The connection between a particular crystal and a chakra is based on the colour of the crystal and on its vibration or subtle electromagnetic field. Generally, crystals with a lower vibration heal conditions related to the lower chakras, while crystals with a higher vibration work best on conditions associated with the upper chakras.

To choose a crystal for healing a particular problem, the chart on pages 108–109 is a good place to start. But you can also trust your own intuition. Simply hold the crystal in your hand, close your eyes and ask yourself: "Where in my body do I feel this crystal's vibration?" A subtle tingling in the middle of your chest, for instance, signals a crystal you can use to balance your heart chakra and relieve heart-chakra related conditions.

For healing, place the crystal you have chosen directly on the affected part of your body or hold the crystal in your hand and gently massage the area. Wearing a crystal ring or pendant keeps the crystal's energy with you throughout your busy day. You can also use the crystal to make a gem remedy to enhance a healing evening bath.

***CRYSTAL HEALING BATH***
*In the morning, place a clean crystal in a glass bowl. Fill the bowl with spring water. Allow the bowl to stand on a sunny windowsill or outside in the garden during the day. In the evening, remove the crystal and add the gem-infused water to your bath.*

# Crystals for healing

This chart lists a variety of crystals for healing each chakra. Use the healing tips suggested or let them inspire your own crystal healing therapies.

| CHAKRA | CRYSTALS |
| --- | --- |
| *Root* | *Smoky quartz, garnet, bloodstone, ruby, red jasper, red beryl, red calcite* |
| *Sacral* | *Orange carnelian, orange calcite, citrine, tangerine quartz, fire opal* |
| *Solar plexus* | *Malachite, amber, yellow jasper, yellow tourmaline, rhodochrosite, golden topaz, tiger's eye, citrine* |
| *Heart* | *Rose quartz, chrysophase, pink tourmaline, peridot, green aventurine, jade* |
| *Throat* | *Turquoise, lapis lazuli, aquamarine, blue lace agate, celestite, blue sapphire, sodalite* |
| *Brow* | *Amethyst, sodalite, moldavite, azurite, purple fluorite, lilac kunzite, electric blue obsidian* |
| *Crown* | *Amber, purple jasper, purple sapphire, clear quartz, diamond, amethyst, lilac danburite, labradorite (spectorolite)* |

## HEALING TIPS

*Carry a piece of red calcite in the pocket of your jeans to loosen your joints and relieve hip and lower limb problems.*

*Add a gem remedy made with orange calcite to your evening bath to balance your emotions and heal reproductive system ills.*

*Place a piece of malachite on your solar plexus to balance your blood sugar, strengthen your abdominal organs, and relieve nausea caused by travel sickness.*

*Wear a jade pendant to help resolve relationship difficulties by releasing feelings of irritation, encouraging harmony, and increasing your ability to love.*

*Gently massage your throat chakra with a polished piece of lapis lazuli before you give a talk to stimulate honest and powerful self-expression.*

*Tape a flat piece of moldavite to your forehead before going to sleep to invite a dream that gives you insight into the past causes of an illness or health condition.*

*Hold a piece of clear quartz in your hands during your bedtime meditation to harmonize all of your chakras and strengthen your immune system.*

# Crystal layout

Placing crystals directly on your chakra points is a powerful way to cleanse, balance, and recharge your chakra energies. The basic layout technique, right, can be used to work on all of your chakras at once to relieve a condition affecting your whole body or as a preventive measure. Or, you can adapt the technique to focus on healing a condition associated with a particular chakra.

**CRYSTAL HEALING LAYOUT**

*1. Gather the crystals you will use for your layout and cleanse them by holding them under running water. Allowing washed crystals to dry in the sun will enhance their energy, so dry them in the sun whenever possible.*

*2. Lie on your back on a yoga mat or folded blanket.*

*3. Place the crystals on your chakras as shown, starting with the root chakra. The crystals listed below are easy to obtain as tumbled or polished stones and are not expensive, but feel free to substitute other crystals from the chart on pages 108–109 for the suggested crystals. If you are strongly attracted to a particular crystal, follow your intuition and use it as part of your layout.*

- *Place red jasper on your root chakra.*
- *Place orange carnelian on your sacral chakra.*
- *Place citrine on your solar plexus chakra.*
- *Place green aventurine on your heart chakra.*

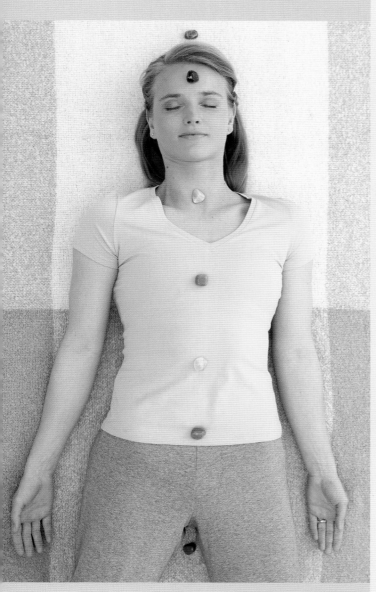

- *Place blue lace agate on your throat chakra.*
- *Place sodalite on your brow chakra.*
- *Place amethyst just above the top of your head for your crown chakra.*

4. As you place each crystal on your body, focus your attention for several minutes on the chakra point being targeted. Remind yourself that the crystal's vibration is resonating with your own life energy, cleansing, balancing, and healing.

5. Allow 20 minutes for the crystals to do their work.

6. Always cleanse your crystals after using them for healing by holding them under running water, as you did before starting this healing layout.

# Chakra therapy

Illness is most likely to be caused by a combination of mental, physical, and energetic factors. Stress is known to contribute to heart disease. Stiffness in the joints may indicate rigid attitudes as well as arthritis. In this section, you'll find chakra healing techniques for common ailments. Addressing a problem's energetic causes can be a useful part of any treatment plan.

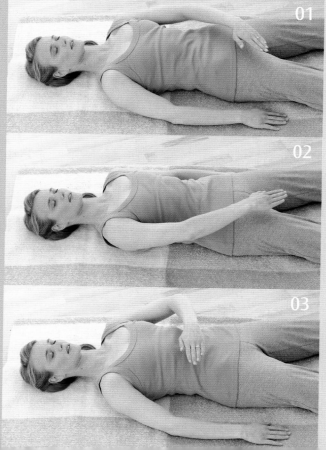

01

02

03

### FIGHTING A COLD OR INFECTION

*Using your hands to enhance the spin of your chakras helps to pull out toxic energies and strengthen your immune system to help you fight off a cold or other infection.*

*(01) Lie on your back on a yoga mat or folded blanket. Using your left hand, begin to circle it about 10 cm (4 in) above your root chakra in a slow anticlockwise (counterclockwise) motion. Your circles should be about the width of your body. Continue for about 3–4 minutes. The anticlockwise circles pull out stagnant or negative energy.*

*(02) Then, using your right hand, reverse the motion and circle 10 cm (4 in) above the root chakra in a slow clockwise motion. Continue for about 1–2 minutes. The clockwise circles strengthen the chakra's natural spin.*

*(03) Moving up your body, repeat these slow circular motions in both directions 10 cm (4 in) above your sacral, solar plexus, heart, and throat chakras.*

## CRYSTAL HEALING FOR HEADACHES

*Amethyst crystals are powerful healers for ills influenced by the brow and crown chakras. Two techniques are offered here – experiment with both. Chronic headaches, including migraines, tend to respond better to the alternate technique included here also.*

*1. Lie down on a yoga mat or folded blanket. Place a flat pillow under your head to ease tension in your neck.*

*2. Place a small tumbled amethyst crystal on your forehead as near as possible to the spot where you feel the pain.*

**Alternative:** *place a small, single-terminated amethyst crystal underneath your head at the base of your skull, with the termination pointing toward your feet.*

*3. Close your eyes and follow your breathing all the way in and all the way out. Relax your muscles starting with your feet and working your way up your body. Pay special attention to relaxing any tension that has built up in your face, particularly your mouth and jaw.*

*4. Allow about 20 minutes for the amethyst to do its work. Be sure to cleanse the crystal after use (see Crystal healing layout p. 110).*

### AROMATHERAPY FOR A SORE THROAT OR COUGH
*Breathing in steam infused with essential oils is a natural therapy for ailments connected to the throat chakra, such as a sore throat, cold, or cough.*

*1. Half fill a bowl with boiling water and add to it 4–5 drops of one of these essential oils: for sore throat, thyme, rosewood, lavender, or sandalwood; for a cough, bergamot, myrtle, thyme, or sandalwood; and for a cold, eucalyptus or rosemary.*

*2. Bend over the bowl and cover your head with a towel. Breathe in the aromatic steam deeply through your nose for a few minutes. Repeat up to five times in any one day.*

*3. If you must go to work, put a few drops of eucalyptus oil on a tissue and breathe in the soothing fragrance throughout the day.*

*4. In the evening, sprinkle a few drops of one of the essential oils mentioned above into your bathwater and relax as you breathe in the healing fragrance.*

## SUN BREATH FOR PRE-MENSTRUAL TENSION

*The golden-orange light of the sun is a great natural source of healing for ailments connected to the sacral chakra, including pre-menstrual tension and infertility. Try this exercise in the morning when the vital energy of the sun is most potent or during a lunchtime stroll in the park.*

*1. Stand facing the sun with your feet one shoulder-width apart. Bring your attention to your sacral chakra. Imagine that you can breathe the energy of the sun into your chakra, filling it with golden-orange light.*

*2. Inhale the golden-orange energy through your nose and draw it down gently to your sacral chakra. Remind yourself that as the sunlight balances and heals your chakra, it is also balancing and strengthening reproductive system organs.*

*3. Visualize that any pain, discomfort, blockages, or upsets to your reproductive system are leaving your body with every out-breath.*

*4. Continue this visualization for about three minutes, until you feel energized and relaxed.*

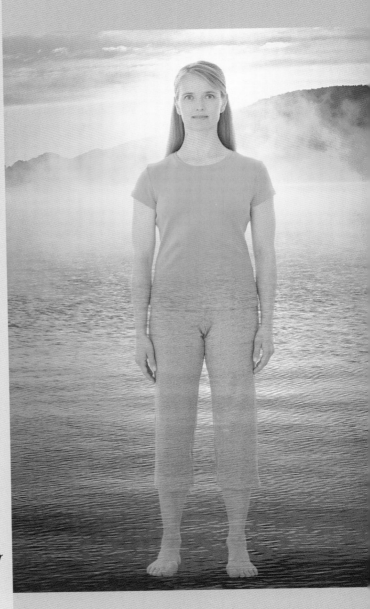

# Chakra toning for health

Toning is vocalizing the sound of a vowel without melody or rhythm. The vowel sounds associated with the chakras are based on Sanskrit and are found in most languages around the world. As you extend the vowel sound with your voice, the vibration of your breath massages your body from the inside out, relieving tension and stress, balancing the energy of your chakras, and promoting health and well-being.

If you can use a piano to find the right note, or if you have musical knowledge, vocalizing each sound on the appropriate note makes toning even more powerful and effective. Here are the traditional correspondences between the chakras and vowel sounds.

| *CHAKRAS AND MUSIC* | | |
| --- | --- | --- |
| *Chakra* | *Vowel sound* | *Musical note* |
| Root | "uh" as in "cup" | C |
| Sacral | "oo" as in "you" | D |
| Solar plexus | "oh" as in "go" | E |
| Heart | "ah" as in "ma" | F |
| Throat | "iy" as in "eye" | G |
| Brow | "ay" as in "pray" | A |
| Crown | "ee" as in "we" | B |

## VOCAL TONING

*Use this basic toning technique every morning or evening to maintain good health and vitality. Move upward through the chakras, toning each vowel sound for 2–3 minutes. Your toning session should not last longer than 20 minutes.*

*(01) Sit comfortably on a chair or on a cushion on the floor. Try to keep your back as straight as possible to allow the energy to flow easily through your channels. Relax, especially your tongue and your jaw. Make each sound several times (see left), starting with "uh" for the root chakra. Stop to inhale whenever you need to. Use a gentle voice and don't strain. Allow the sound to ride your breath, expanding the sound to a moderate loudness.*

*(02) Move upward through the chakras. If you feel any tension in your mouth or neck, stop to yawn, stretch, or swallow. It's also useful to have a glass of water nearby in case your throat gets dry.*

# CHAPTER SIX

# Chakra relaxation

During your day, your body's energy system has worked hard, adjusting to intensity, stress, vitality, focus, pleasure, and healing. Clearing and closing down your chakras is a great way to settle your body and mind for a restful night's sleep.

Evening is also an ideal time to lay aside your everyday responsibilities and concerns and open yourself to dreams and intuition. The brow chakra, located between your physical eyes, governs your ability to see – both physical sight and the internal images you get from memories, dreams, and intuitive insights. Working with your brow chakra enhances your ability to envision your life and to use your dreams and intuitive perceptions for helpful advice and guidance.

Your crown chakra, located at the top of the head, controls thought, consciousness, and understanding, including spiritual understanding and your connection to faith in a higher power. Just as you began your day by working with your root chakra to strengthen your grounded connection to the earth, ending your day with a crown chakra meditation strengthens your connection to spirit. A before-bed session of meditation completes your daily journey through the chakras and brings your energy body into peaceful alignment.

# Relax and scan

The first part of your evening routine might focus on simply unwinding from the busy events of the day. Any activity that helps you relax and review how the day went for you is a useful way to close down your energy.

You might find it helpful to write in your journal, not to congratulate yourself for your successes or beat yourself up for your shortcomings, but simply to bring a sense of completeness to the day's activities. Pay special attention to thinking and writing about how well you managed your energy during the course of the day and what you might do tomorrow to better it. For instance, if you found it difficult to be energetic and focused after lunch, consider whether you might try different foods or different companions, or whether you might make time after lunch for a refreshing walk.

Another good unwinding activity is curling up in your favourite chair with a cup of lavender or some other relaxing herbal tea. Lavender is also a favourite calming fragrance to add to an evening bath. The purple colour of lavender flowers harmonizes well with the energy of the brow and crown chakras.

As you sip your herbal tea or relax in an aromatic bath, take a moment to scan your chakras, using the same technique you used in the morning to awaken your energy body (see pages 32–33). Focus your attention inward and gently allow your mind to travel to each chakra in turn, this time starting with the crown chakra and moving downward to the root chakra. As you scan your chakras, pay attention to any images, memories or feelings from the day that arise and gently let them go.

## RELAXING HERBAL TEAS

### Chamomile
Known for its mild, apple-like flavour, chamomile relieves restlessness, nervousness, tension, and mild insomnia.

### Valerian
This calming herb helps to promote sleep without the risk of a morning hangover that can result from using sleep medicines.

### Lavender
This soothing and aromatic tea has a light and slightly sweet taste. A cup before bed promotes restful sleep. Blend lavender with mint leaves for an extra refreshing treat.

### Lemon balm
Lemon balm tea has been used since the Middle Ages to relax the nerves and relieve anxiety.

### Sage
This aromatic tea helps to relieve tension headaches, digestive discomforts, and stomach cramps that may interfere with restful sleep.

# Relaxing yoga

These simple exercises drawn from yoga can help you
clear and balance your chakras as part of your evening
relaxation routine.

### *STRETCHES*

*(01) Stand with your feet parallel and
shoulder-width apart. As you inhale, raise
your arms above your head, straighten them,
and clasp your hands together, palms facing
upward. Rise up on your toes and stretch your
whole body upward. Keep your shoulders
down and engage the muscles between your
shoulder blades as you stretch. As you exhale,
return your arms to your sides and lower your
heels to the floor. Repeat twice more.*

*(02) Next, raise your arms over your head. Bend
over to one side, hold your position for a few
seconds and then return to an upright position.
Then bend to the other side and return to
centre. Repeat twice more to each side.*

*(03) Finally, stand comfortably and inhale.
As you exhale, bend forward from your waist,
stretching your fingers toward your toes. Allow
your head to hang down easily. Come back to
standing. Then repeat twice more.*

## SUPPORTED CHILD POSE

1. Sit on your heels with your knees wide apart. Bend forward and rest your abdomen, chest, and head on a bolster pillow or stack of folded towels. You should be high enough that your upper body is parallel to the floor.

2. Your arms should lie comfortably to each side of the pillow, resting on the floor from the elbows to the fingertips, your elbows in line with your shoulders.

3. Your head should be turned to one side to rest on one cheek.

4. As you breathe, pay attention to the soothing way your solar plexus, heart, and throat chakras are supported by the pillow. Feel the gentle massage your inhalations and exhalations give to the area around each of your chakras. Remain in this position for up to five minutes, allowing all thoughts, emotions, and physical tension to drain away.

# Clearing, closing, and protecting

Clearing your chakras of accumulated impressions from the activities of your day and gently closing down their energy helps you to relax deeply and prepare for sleep. As a final step, you wrap yourself in a comforting blanket of protection that keeps your energy body balanced and safe throughout the night.

This exercise, like others in this book, uses the power of visualization, governed by the brow chakra, to achieve the desired result. There's nothing mysterious about visualization. You are always seeing images on the screen of your mind – memories, dreams, creative projects, even how a recipe you are preparing for dinner will look on the plate.

You can strengthen your ability to visualize by mentally reviewing the scenes and events of your day. Close your eyes and bring to mind a vivid picture of the clothes you wore; what you ate for breakfast; a significant event or conversation. Bringing these memories to life on the screen of your mind engages and empowers the energy of your brow chakra.

Practising visualization exercises as part of your evening relaxation routine also strengthens your ability to create and recall internal imagery, which helps you to make your dreams more vivid and much more memorable.

**CLEARING**
*The first part of this sequence helps to clear your chakras of the excess energy that has built up from the events of your busy day by washing it away with a refreshing visualized shower.*

*1. Stand easily with your feet slightly apart. Relax your body and breathe through your nose.*

*2. On the screen of your mind, see yourself standing under a shower of sparkling silver light. Feel free to use your imagination to see light as a refreshing shower of rain-drops or as the gentle cascade of a tropical waterfall.*

*3. The silver shower splashes over your body, washing away the energetic impressions of your day's activities. See any unwanted energy that may have become entangled in your aura being swept away and disappearing into the ground under your feet.*

4. Imagine further that the silver shower washes not only the outside of your body but also the inside. It enters through your crown chakra and flows through your energy body, washing away any blockages and debris from your channels and chakras. All unwanted energy pours out through the soles of your feet and disappears into the ground, like dirty dishwater swirling down the drain.

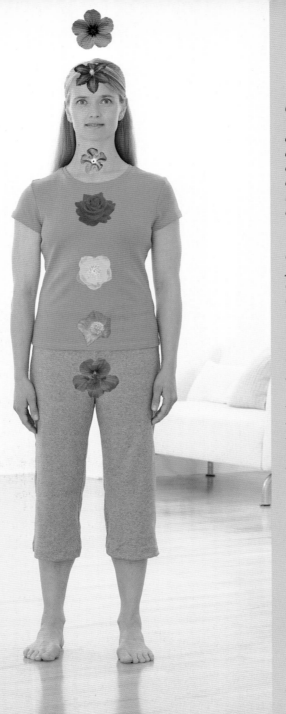

## CLOSING

*When you feel that your energy body is cleared, you are ready to close down your chakras. You don't want to close your chakras completely, but simply to turn down their energy so you can sleep well.*

*1. Imagine that each of your chakras is a fully opened flower in its appropriate colour. Traditionally, the chakras are visualized as lotus flowers, but it's fine to use any flowers you like. For instance, your solar plexus chakra can be a daffodil and your heart chakra, a rose.*

*2. Focus your attention on your crown chakra, which you see as a violet flower with open petals. On the screen of your mind, visualize that the petals of the flower are closing up a little.*

*3. Then move down to the brow chakra, which you see as an indigo coloured flower. See its petals close slightly.*

*4. Use the same procedure to close down the flower of each of your chakras.*

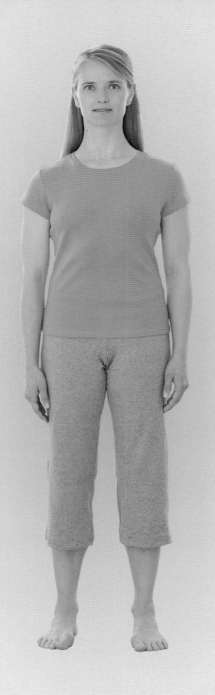

## PROTECTING

*As a final step, you surround yourself with a soothing and protective blanket of light energy, which stays in place throughout the night.*

*1. Now imagine that you can wrap yourself in a comforting sphere of coloured light. Trust your intuition to decide what colour the light should be. If you feel the need of warmth, the light can be a warm red or a sunny orange-gold. If you prefer lightness and coolness, imagine that the light is turquoise or violet.*

*2. As you breathe in, focus on the coloured light and imagine it is spreading from under your feet and up the front of your body. Breathe the light up your body to the top of your head. As you breathe out, imagine that the light is spreading over the top of your head, and then down your back until it connects with itself under your feet, enclosing your entire body in a sphere of energetic protection.*

# Special focus: the brow chakra

In Sanskrit, the brow chakra is called *ajna*, which means both "to perceive" and "to command". Also known as the "third eye", the purpose of this chakra is to help you take command of your life by giving you the tools of vision, intuition, and insight.

On the physical level, the brow chakra influences your eyes and your ability to see. Problems with the brow chakra can lead to eyestrain, headaches, and migraine. You may also have memory problems, nightmares, troubling dreams, or insomnia.

But generally, the brow chakra governs mental rather than physical qualities. When your brow chakra is weak, you are more likely to have difficulty perceiving yourself and others clearly. When you are unable to see the consequences of your own actions or the true intentions of people in your life, you are more likely to blame others for your problems.

A strong brow chakra, on the other hand, gives you the ability to discern the patterns and colours of life clearly – both on the physical level and with your mind. You see how events and people fit together in the greater pattern of life and understand your place in the grand design. With the gift of insight into yourself and others, you can expand the "gut feelings" you get from your solar plexus chakra into intuitive knowledge that you can use to make wise life decisions. You also find it easy to use the inner screen of your mind to envision clearly what you want to accomplish.

Finally, a healthy brow chakra widens your perception so that you can understand your dreams and use them as a source of insight and guidance.

> reas

## METHODS FOR STRENGTHENING YOUR BROW CHAKRA

| Where to focus | What to do |
| --- | --- |
| Foods | Drink herbal teas, including peppermint to stimulate intuition, and sage to encourage powerful and vivid dreams. |
| Colour therapy | Grow a pot of African violets on your bedroom windowsill; plant iris bulbs in your garden. |
| Aromatherapy | Put a few drops of violet, rose or geranium essential oil into your evening bath to calm and soothe a troubled mind. |
| Crystals | Place an amethyst crystal under your pillow to protect against nightmares and insomnia. |
| Clothes | Try some new eye make-up; update the look of your glasses, or buy a beautiful new pair of sunglasses. |
| Self-care | Get your eyes checked; keep a notebook and pen on your bedside table so that you can write down your dreams. |
| Recreation | See or create something colourful and beautiful – visit a gallery or art museum; get out your watercolours and paint a landscape or a vase of flowers. |
| House and home | Pay special attention to adding vivid colours and interesting patterns to your home décor. |
| Journal exercise | Write about: what do I see myself doing in five years? What is my vision for my future career, home, relationship? How has intuition helped me to make good decisions? |

# Star gazing

As your brow chakra grows stronger, so does your ability to use your intuition to "see" into problems in your life. With a little practice, you can train yourself to use your wisdom eye to gain insight into your life's deep patterns and even to glimpse your future.

Many of the exercises in this book have given you practice in visualizing images on the screen of your mind. This exercise widens your screen to the vast expanse of the starry night sky. If you do not live in a place where the stars are easily visible, or if the weather is too cold for stargazing, try this same technique while lying on your back in bed imagining that the ceiling of your bedroom is a movie screen.

**VISUALIZING WITH THE STARS**

*1. Choose a clear night when the weather is comfortable for you to be outside. Prepare a place where you can lie on your back, or sit if you prefer, and be cozy, warm, and dry. If possible, choose a spot away from city lights. Bring a warm jacket or wrap yourself in a blanket or shawl.*

*2. Stretch out under the stars and spend a few minutes following your breath. Allow yourself to "fall into the night sky", becoming aware of its fathomless depths.*

*3. Gently turn your mind to some problem or situation in your life into which you would like insight. Allow whatever you need to see about this situation to be revealed on the vast screen of the sky.*

*4. If it feels appropriate, ask for a vision that gives you insight into the deeper patterns of your life – what you came into this life to accomplish and what still needs to be done.*

# Decoding your dreams

To decode the messages of your dreams, it's important to write them down. Keep a notebook and pen next to your bed, and write down whatever you remember as soon as you awaken. Writing down your dreams not only strengthens the energy of your brow chakra, it also increases your ability to recall dream images.

At least once a week, set aside some time during your evening relaxation routine to work with the dreams you've recorded. Here are some guidelines:

■ Pay attention to the details. Assume that every person, place, colour, sound, situation, and event in your dream is trying to convey an important message about you or your life. Look for recurring patterns, such as a series of dreams with similar images. Pay attention to colours, sounds, and smells. Describe as clearly as you can your emotions during the dream and how you felt when you woke up.
■ Begin to decode a dream by making a list of personal associations and connections with the dream's images. Write down any words, memories, feelings, or ideas that are triggered by the people, places, events, and sensations in your dream.
■ To find the message, use the screen of your mind to dialogue with dream characters. Ask them questions, such as: Who are you? What part of me do you represent? How do I feel about you? Also ask yourself questions about dream details, such as: What do I have in common with that? Where have I seen that in my life? What feelings does that bring up? Make notes about what you discover.

**CLUES**
*The most useful way to think about the characters and situations you encounter in dreams is as clues to hidden aspects of your self.*

■ Finally, use your intuition to put the pieces together. Ask yourself: What is this dream trying to tell me? What is its advice or guidance? Don't expect the meaning of your dreams to be clear immediately. You'll know you are on the right track when the message you get gives you fresh insight into yourself or a sudden surge of life energy.

**DREAM**
*Though the images in your dreams may seem weird and confusing, working with them patiently can provide helpful insights.*

# Special focus: the crown chakra

The Sanskrit name for the crown chakra is *sahasrara*, which means "thousandfold". The name refers to the traditional comparison of your spiritual consciousness to a lotus flower with a thousand petals, a symbol of the many ways you can reach out to Divine energy.

The crown chakra governs consciousness itself – your ability to think, reason, analyze, learn, and know. Located on the top of the head, or in some belief systems, just above the top of the head, the crown chakra helps you to integrate the perceptions, emotions, and experiences governed by the other six chakras and bring them into harmonious balance and alignment. Though the colour usually associated with the crown chakra is violet, it is also sometimes visualized as white, which is actually the combination of all other colours.

Any spiritual activity that feels right to you can help to strengthen your crown chakra, including prayer, meditation, yoga, and spiritual reading or study. When your own energy system is aligned, these activities can more easily expand your everyday mind so that it is able to experience higher states of consciousness, such as spiritual bliss, mystical understanding, and inner peace.

When you make time each day to balance and align your own energy, regular spiritual practice becomes an important, joyful, and fulfilling part of every day life. Just as the root chakra grounds you in material reality, the crown chakra opens you up like a thousand-petalled lotus so that you can appreciate spiritual reality – the Divine spark within you and your profound connection to all that is.

## METHODS FOR STRENGTHENING YOUR CROWN CHAKRA

| Where to focus | What to do |
| --- | --- |
| Foods | None; if your health permits, try fasting for a day as you focus on meditation, dream work, and other consciousness expanding activities. |
| Colour therapy | Visualize that a heavenly white or violet/purple light is pouring down into the top of your head. |
| Aromatherapy | Light a stick of frankincense, myrrh, or sandalwood incense when you sit down to pray or meditate. |
| Crystals | Place a beautiful piece of clear quartz near your favourite spiritual picture or statue. |
| Clothes | Wear a purple shirt or sweater with a white skirt or trousers. |
| Self-care | Turn off the computer and the TV and refresh your spirit with a day of silence and reflection. |
| Recreation | Sign up for a class in meditation, yoga, tai chi, or other spiritual discipline you've always wanted to try. |
| House and home | Create a restful and beautiful meditation space for doing spiritual work at home. |
| Journal exercise | Write about: what are my spiritual beliefs? What could I do to deepen my spiritual understanding? |

# Spiritual connections

If your personal connection to God or your higher power was stronger at some earlier point in your life, such as when you were a child, and you would like to reestablish that link, engaging the energy of your crown chakra can help. If your connection to a higher power is as strong now as it ever was, your crown chakra can help you add intensity and focus to your end-of-day prayers.

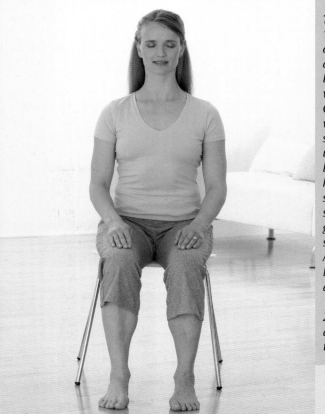

**THE SILVER THREAD**
*1. Sit comfortably in a chair or on the floor. Relax and allow your memory to travel back to a time in your life when your connection to God or your higher power was particularly vital. Allow specific memories to arise, using all of your senses to bring the scenes to life: the light streaming though a stained glass window; the smell of moist earth in a grove of ancient trees, the sweet harmony of a choir. Allow the emotions triggered by these memories to warm and open your heart.*

*2. Now, from your open heart, ask God or your higher power to help you come into closer*

connection. As you do this, imagine that a beam of light, like a shining silver thread, emerges from the centre of your crown chakra and reaches directly to God or your higher power.

3. At the end of this thread is a silver hook. Miraculously, the hook catches hold of you connecting you and your higher power with a most powerful bond.

4. The silver thread can stay connected for as long as you wish. Use it like a telephone wire to send specific prayers for yourself, for people in your life or for all beings. Use it to receive messages of unconditional compassion and love sent from your higher power to you.

5. When your prayers are complete, allow the silver thread and its hook to dissolve, knowing that you can reconnect it whenever you wish.

### END OF DAY MEDITATION
*In Buddhism, when your last thoughts before falling asleep are spiritual in nature, the hours you spend sleeping can be transformed into a positive opportunity for spiritual connection.*

*1. Sit comfortably on a pillow on the floor, or if you prefer, upright in bed with pillows behind your back.*

*2. Relax your body and breathe slowly and deeply through your nose for a few moments, following your breathing all the way in and all the way out.*

*3. Turn your attention to your root chakra. Ask this part of your being to ground your spiritual practice with solid support and steadiness.*

*4. Turn your attention to your sacral chakra. Ask this part of your being to fuel and fire your spiritual passion.*

*5. Turn your attention to your solar plexus chakra. Ask this part of your being to give powerful focus to both your prayers and meditations.*

6. Turn your attention to your heart chakra. Ask this part of your being to open you to universal and unconditional love and compassion.

7. Turn your attention to your throat chakra. Ask this part of your being to help your consciousness communicate with Divine consciousness.

8. Turn your attention to your brow chakra. Ask this part of your being to inspire you with spiritual vision and insight.

9. Now, turn your attention to your crown chakra. Visualize it as a fully opened white flower with a thousand petals. Imagine that from each petal a stream of light extends upward to the source of Divine light. Imagine further that light is flowing both upward from your crown to the source and downward from the source into you, filling you from toe to crown with understanding, wisdom, and peace.

# Index